HD Life

Living Your Life In High Definition

Milton Howard, Jr.

See More Than What Is Seen !
Then Relate To The More
And Not The Less!

Milton Howard, Jr.

HD Life

ISBN 978-1479308187

Table of Contents

HD Life

The High Definition Life. The word Definition can be and should be one of the most important word concepts in your life. The power to define is what sets you and I apart from the rest of existence, which includes the plant and animal life and all that's contained in the Universe that's living. We are gifted with this super phenomenon of being able to map out, choose, create, and develop on purpose, and without that knowledge, life is left to the game of chance, and your life will be left to the will and design of forces outside of yourself. This knowledge is the awareness of and the ability to focus on the gift to define.

HD Life is about seeing your life magnified with clarity. Sometimes because so much remains unclear, it becomes hard to discover those things in your life that are either helping you or even those things in life that might be hindering you. The power to define gives you the edge you need to organize the elements within your life that can create a dynamic platform to develop all the desires you can ever imagine and hope for.

Developing Versus Receiving

You must make it a point to take and make specific time to define your life, define your goals, define your dreams, define your relationships, and everything else about you. Definition must come from you. Again, the power to define gives you the edge you need to organize the elements within your life that can create a dynamic platform to develop all the desires you can ever imagine and hope for.

Now I could have written the last sentence like this, " The power to define gives you the edge you need to organize what is in your life that creates a platform to receive all the desires you can ever imagine or hope for." Here I used the word "receive" instead of using the word "develop". Did you notice that major word change? Do you not receive all the desires you can ever imagine or hope for? You don't. You have to develop them.

What I'm going to do here now is give you some history about "you" in order for you to better understand the need to have a High Definition life. Once I complete this history, it is my desire that you gain a greater ability to know and recognize that everything, or better yet, "every-thing" that you need to accomplish anything in life, you already have within you. This is not the latest religious statement or motivational feel good phrase. I really want to paint a vivid picture in your mind that will bring to the forefront of your understanding that all the money, dynamic relationships, health, and the desires you could ever want in life, you already have. What might be missing here is the experience of those things or even the ability to see those things in order to gain the experience. The knowledge and understanding of what exist in you is the beginning of experience. If I can prove this fact, then there will be no need to "receive" anything in your life, just a need to develop them.

"Every-thing" that you need to accomplish "Any-thing", you already have within you.

When you think in terms of receiving, you also reach a corresponding conclusion that whatever you desire is not there, thus the need to receive. This is why it is dangerous to think in terms of receiving because it knocks out of your mind the reality of what is in existence within you. I would like to direct your consciousness to this fact and reinforce the same fact, that is, when you become conscious of your desire; the entirety of that desire resides in you. Literally, it geographically resides in you as a living entity in the smallest of formations, so with this, information has immediately taken on formation within you. When you accept this fact, it forces you to begin to structure the contents of your desire even though the physical reality is in its smallest formation. Thoughts are literally things that sets itself within you as desire, which is a literal, physical existence. Then you "develop" what already exist.

Yes, I am saying, take responsibility for your personal development. Don't wait for things to happen or wait for things to come to you. You have the ability to respond to your own desire and begin development. First, by organizing your thoughts, and secondly, by constructing your feelings that correspond to those thoughts. Not feelings that respond, but feelings that correspond. Third, as your corresponding feelings send out the aura of your reality, people in your life should be set to respond to what is corresponded in you. This is the building of the first body that brings the life imbedded within you into a more physical reality. You must have people around you that agree with your desire. Lastly, both you and the people who respond to the truth within you must consistently act towards this truth.

Take responsibility for your personal development.

In having a High Definition lifestyle, you must magnify the things in your life that already exist which is placed within you for your benefit. Therefore, with the very things you desire to have and do in life being in existence already, you must now approach life with the notion of development and not the notion of receiving. You must also "X" out the notion of waiting for people to change to match your desire. People around you must have enough respect for you to see what's in you and begin to enhance that dynamic formulation within you immediately. But sometimes we sit around and wait for people to see our good and then respond to our good. We wait for them to change their behavior towards us versus dealing with people who already match our desires.

Here we go.

Results Now from Then

No one can really argue that behind everything that exists, by the shear fact of its amazing construction, from plant life, to animal life, to life in the sea, and to life contained within this awe-striking universe which includes the celestial stars, planets, moons, galaxies and solar systems, there must be a definite Intelligence behind the order of things. A good percentage of the religious world has an epic version of the creation story in some form or another. Scientists view the origin of life with the Big Bang theory as its base. As for me, I have no arguments against either. Everybody is still trying to figure this out and that's ok.

In my attempt to trace down the origin of things and the origin of life, I would like to start with the life we have now as human beings. We as human beings are incredible creatures. The physical make-up of our bodies alone is astounding. Now add to this the fact that human beings have the capacity to think.

Hmmmmm?

Here are creatures on Earth with the most ingenious physical make-up in existence with the capacity to think, to create thoughts, and to birth ideas. Not only can we create thoughts, but those very thoughts can be developed to the point to where what we think will organize the surrounding substances in such a way that we then begin to experience what we think from a physical standpoint. In other words, what we think becomes our experience as it is developed out of the pre-existing sub-stances that are designed to support our thought processes.

Case in point.

Let's take Sam Walton, the founder of the massive trillion-dollar retail chain, Wal-Mart. The initial thought for this retail giant was birthed out of the dissatisfaction with a local "5 and dime" store in his small-town community. As his thought developed further, he decided to correct the issues by developing his own retail outlet. The story extends from "then" to "now", where now there exists a trillion-dollar entity that serves millions of people every day. Before Sam Walton passed away, he was able to walk into any one of his hundreds of stores and experience something that was once just a thought in his mind.

Everything in life that we experience whether good or bad has its origin in our minds, whether we are conscious of it or not. Our very own unique Intelligence provides for everything we experience in life. Notice that there is a "then" and "now" to everything that exist. Sam Walton opened his first Wal-Mart in 1962. His first "5 and dime" store was purchased in 1950. So, his "then" began before 1950 within his mind and is "now" is worth billions.

Let's look at it from this viewpoint.

What happened "then" when the Universe began? There had to be a thought behind it. Therefore, based on the order of things that happened immediately after the first moments of the Universe, there must have been Intelligence "then" so that the same Intelligence or

Thought could experience results "now". Our "now" proves emphatically that there was a "then" that was steeped in a thought process.

The experience of results is the express reason for your existence. You were created to be successful. You were created to grow. Life is meant to be enjoyed, and to enjoy life you must have things to experience, and the best way to ensure good experiences is to use your gift of intelligence to define your life.

The experience of results is the express reason for your existence.

The fact that you and I are an intelligent, thinking, thoughtful being proves that Intelligence exists. You would also need to accept this as a statement of faith, that you are part of the same Intelligence that existed before the Universe began. Consciousness of the Intelligence that defines you might not be readily available to your mind at this point, but it can be. That's why it is incredibly important for you to view your life from the standpoint of High Definition.

OK. Let's turn our attention back to development.

The Concept of Development

Again, most people view life from the standpoint of receiving the things in life that they want, and this is very understandable. People work and then receive a paycheck. Children participate in school and receive a grade. Be a good boy or good girl and receive presents on Christmas day from Santa. Go to church and do all the right things and receive a blessing. Do a good job at work and receive a raise. This process of receiving sets up an emotion of expectation for things coming to you based on your behavior patterns.

But this pattern is generally not guaranteed as many people experience what they consider to be bad luck, because the system doesn't seem to be fair at times in giving them what they want in life. If you think from within this type of system of receiving, things will not always be fair because here, you have no control.

A system that is a 100% accurate is the system of development and not the system of receiving. Here the focus shifts from receiving what you might think is coming to you and switching to developing everything within you that already exists. This also includes love. You do not receive love. You develop love. Now, who agrees with the love in you? This again requires a High Definition life.

Most agree that the Universe began in an instant. Here, I must take this opportunity to present to the Christian thinker that the Biblical account of creation states the exact same thing. The Universe in an instant? Once you look at it a little closer, the Universe began in an instant and everything after that was subsequently developed from that point.

If the Genesis account is read and understood correctly, you will come to know that creation was just a moment in time. Once the Creation came into existence, God spent the other six days or time expanses developing what was created, developing what was in existence, developing what came into existence in one moment in time. Here the concept of development was set as an archetype and can serve as a model as to how you can gain all of your personal desires.

The Biblical text reads, "In the beginning God created the heavens and the Earth".

Done!

Then immediately after that, throughout the Christian account of Genesis, God divided things that existed to make and develop new formations of things. Science itself proves that everything in existence is constructed from one substance that now exists in different formations. The periodic chart and the arrangements of the elements via the placement of protons, neutrons, and electrons eloquently display this concept. But notice here, what differentiates one element from another is their arrangement, how they were developed in time and over time.

What does any of this have to do with you living a better life, achieving higher goals, and having all of your desires?

You are an "arranger". You are a developer! Because you have intelligence, you can arrange anything in your life that exist to be what you want it to be. That's what God did, or the Original Intelligence, which is you.

Intelligence Arranged. Placed. Ordered. Intelligence developed that which was in full existence. The fact that you are breathing means that you are in Full Existence also. The fact that you are intelligent means that you can arrange things to be whatever you want them to be. Even when there are disappointments, you have the ability and the power to reappoint what has been disappointed. The difference between the "haves" and the "have-nots" is the extent to where they join themselves to this knowledge, and then to the extent that they activate this simple knowledge into their lives. Success in life is guaranteed when it is not based on what is received by chance, but by what is developed on purpose.

Experience

There is no one on Earth, no one individual on this planet that is incomplete. Your emotions can arrange themselves in a way that can make you feel incomplete. But remember you can feel incomplete because of how the arrangement of emotions within you make you feel, but you yourself actually can never be incomplete. Emotions here are mostly determined by your experience. Very few people know that they can actually design their emotions based on what they think and not their immediate experience. Everything that exist, exist in fullness and exist in its entirety for you to experience in one form or the other. Things might not be arranged in the order in which you might like them to be, but existence is still an institution of entirety, fullness, and completion.

Experience is a function of the mind. You can experience lack, but lack actually doesn't exist. It is the concept of receiving that will give rise to the feeling of lack, thusly setting up the emotions that become that very experience. I can explain this better by using the grading system within the American educational system.

First, if a child has a test with ten questions on it and misses five of those questions, he or she will be considered as being able to only answer 50% of the questions on the test. With the grading system in America, that would be considered an "F". It is this determination that gives the student an inward sense that they missed the other 50% of the test, so the feeling of lack ensues.

Within the Japanese educational system, a student is credited with getting five questions right with five more questions still in progress to be learned. The students are never assessed as missing the other five. The difference between the two systems is just a thought process and not an actual state of existence and the thought process then becomes an emotion, which is the basis of the experience. The last example leaves the student feeling positive and good, even though he missed the same five questions as the student in the first example.

The difference between a person having $100,000.00 and one having $10.00 is not a state of existence, but a state of mind, a thought process. When I see a country with starving children, I don't see a failed country that is without; I see an undeveloped country that with the right thought process can one day feed its people. Development. And guess what? When there is enough of the desired thought in one place, then the existence will begin to match the thoughts. People would then become more aware that plenty is available to develop and experience. Again, our minds can be darkened to what's available to develop, and one of the chief reasons for this is that some tend to look for what can be received and miss the opportunity to develop what's already there.

When you desire something, it doesn't mean that you are missing it; it only means that you are beginning to recognize that it is already there. It takes a High Definition mind to see it and then to begin the process of development.

Let's look at it this way

For the most part, every human being on Earth has equal access to equal resources. No one on Earth is richer than the other in true reality. Just because Bill Gates is worth billions monetarily, he doesn't have greater ownership of the sunshine, or the rain, or the moon, or the air we breathe. We are more equally rich than we give ourselves credit for.

Gold, silver, diamonds, and other precious minerals found in the earth initially cost nothing. It takes human thought and our own made-up system of evaluation to give these minerals its value. It all happens within the mind. Really! Precious minerals actually cost zero dollars. They are free. Just like the air you breathe cost zero dollars. The moon doesn't stay in its orbit based on financial considerations. It doesn't rain more in Seattle because somebody wrote a check for more rain. The sun doesn't rise based on the amount of money someone has in his or her pocket.

Much in the same way, the resources of the mind and spiritual resources are evenly distributed to everyone equally on this planet. No one has more access to the "Mind" than the other. No one is ever limited in their thinking because of their location or financial ranking. You can't go to the grocery store and buy more "mind". Neither can you buy love or receive love. So why do some people hold within them a strong sense of poverty?

Here's the point.

My son's auto-response when he opens our refrigerator door is, "Ma, there's nothing to eat!", he would say with a great sense of panic and pain. And invariably I would make my way to the refrigerator to assess the emergency. But what I see then is a refrigerator full of food. For my son, if what's in the refrigerator is not what he desires to eat, to him it is the same as having no food at all. It's all in the mind.

There is no financial difference between any human in the world, only a mind difference. And the difference is that some can see things within themselves better than others. These people who can "see" then begin to develop those things in which they have a better view of in their mind into physical existence, thus, they have a different life experience. And remember experience is not existence. Every human being has equal existence, but not equal experiences.

There is no financial difference between any human in the world, only a mind difference.

Having a High Definition life is about taking a closer look. Looking a little closer at your life and thusly begin to be amazed at all that there is waiting to be developed. Even millionaires and billionaires will always find more within themselves to continue to develop outside themselves.

True wealth is found within our thoughts and desires. It is here that you and I, and every other person on this planet are equally rich. Let's look for more so we can experience more. The road map to more starts with what I call the Eight Directives of Destiny.

Desire, Define, Design, Determine, Decide, Develop, Destine & then Deal.

After this, new desires are born.

The 8 Directives of Destiny

The 8 Directives of Destiny

Desire
Define
Design
Determine
Decide
Develop
Destine
&
Deal

After this new Desires are born.

The Actions of the 8 Directives of Destiny

Desire
Define what is Desired.
Design the Defined.
Determine your Design.
Decide what is Determined.
Develop what is Decided.
Destine what is Developed.
Deal what is Destined.

After this new Desires are born.

The Statements of the 8 Directives of Destiny

Desire
Desire is the fundament of evolvement.

Define
The power to define is one of the greatest human attributes. Definition is the arrangement of your available supply including your relationships. You will always possess the power to do this. Your relationships are a form of documentation.

Design
This is the basis of quality. Design is the beginning of the replication of great ideas. This starts on paper or any other form of documentation available to you and then continues into your immediate relationships.

Determine
Determine the endpoints to your Design. Never keep your ideas and wants open-ended. Terminate what doesn't work for you.

Decide
Decide to act on your determination. You must go out of your mind. Movement is not mental, it's actual.

Develop
Arrange and construct the structures of your decision.

Destine
Destiny is never reached without motion. It's about motion based on E-motion. What's moving in you also moves outside of you. Drive what's in you. At every possible incremental time period, push your idea to the next level. Reach a new destination. Mark it. Move it.

Deal
Connection is the basis of value. Deal only to those around you who agree with you and your development. This is the basis for expansion and growth.

After this new Desires are born.

The Knowledge of the 8 Directives of Destiny

Desire

For a good number of people and for the most part, a high value is not placed on things. Things are vital to anyone's existence and a good number of religious persuasions from around the world devalue things in order to gain more access to the spirit. The idea of desire is directed to the spiritual and not to the physical. They imply that somehow if you possess too many things, it will distract your mind from the spiritual. Desire is 100% a matter of the physical and is not a virtue of the spirit.

If you ask the question, how did things come into existence? Every "thing" started from what could not be seen as an idea. It is Intelligence that possesses the ability to have an idea. You possess the ability to have an idea. Without ideas it is impossible to produce things. As I stated earlier, the very beginning of our Universe started with a thought, and that very thought had to be in the form of an idea.

From Ideas to Things

All ideas start in the invisible. Not to devalue any religious notion, but any "thing" that exist, first, it cannot be seen and is spirit. Therefore, any "thing" that exists in the unseen is spiritual. Spirit starts in the unseen and makes its way to what can be seen. My definition of anything that is spiritual is anything that is capable of moving from the unseen to what can be seen. This is the process of creation. To create is spiritual. To make something happen is spiritual. To produce is spiritual. To make things and to have things is spiritual. It has less to do with any religion, religious practice, or moving yourself into the spiritual by denying things, and more to do with being able to see in the spirit and create into the physical those same things which are envisioned. Or might I say, In-Vision.

To create, to make something happen,
and to produce is spiritual.

The whole purpose of Universal Intelligence, the whole reason for God is not to remain unseen and invisible. The process of being is based on what is mirrored into physical existence from what exist in the spirit, hence, what exist in the mind. This makes what you think highly valuable. There is an innate human need to mirror thought, and things are thoughts reflected into a tangible reality. People who have few good things generally have few good thoughts. If this became common knowledge, people would pay more attention to the quality of their thoughts.

What you think is highly valuable.

You must pay attention to the quality of your thoughts, because you are designed in such a way that the Universe goes to immediate work to produce what's on your mind. That's why I tell people, "Do not dismiss your desires". What you desire in life is critical. It may be a new house, a new car, owning your own business so you can make millions or even billions of dollars, to have better relationships, or just to improve your overall quality of life. You can have all of these things based on what you decide to do with your desires. If you dismiss your desires based on a low quality of thinking, you immediately dismiss the possibility of having those things. You can't even dismiss your desires for religious reasons.

You must pay attention to the quality of your thoughts.

Growing Desire

The concept of desire has a purpose. Desire is usually based on moving from one state of existence to a better state of existence. This can be born out of being dissatisfied with your current state and then the need to make things better. I can't express enough especially to those of the Christian faith, God is desire. God is growth. God is love. Love is about growing. Growing is moving from one level to the next. God created you to be better than Himself, because you being better moves Him to another level. Desire is the catalyst for growth and the chief element of growing is desire.

Love is about growing.

This is the fundament of evolvement, and for your desires to become real you must define your desires.

Define What's Desired

The power to define is one of the greatest human attributes. This is what separates human beings from the animal kingdom. When something is not right, when something is out of place, when there is a need to make something happen and things are unclear, you are never left at the mercy of "that's just the way things are", which is a bad mental mindset. You can define and redefine. You have the power to determine how things are going to be.

The key here is to not consider the past or the future. Defining is a process that totally happens in the mind. Mind is always present in your body. Definition is not subject to anything outside of the mind, including anything that is physical, any event, whether it is past or future, and it is definitely not subject to what others have to say or other people's opinions. This is a power that belongs solely to you.

Many people believe that when it comes to events, circumstances, and situations, if it seems to happen outside of their personal sphere of influence, it feels as if they have no control over those matters. This is far from the truth. You must begin with the reality of your mind in your body. Yes, that's right, you have to count what is in your physiological mind as a definite reality. Now this might sound to some as being strange, but this is where many people lose in life. What's in the mind has a greater reality-value than the things you can actually see, hear, taste, smell and feel. Your body is the first reality of your mind.

What's in the mind has a greater physical reality.

What?

Experience and Existence

Yes. Nothing that you can experience with the five senses can be a reality without the mind. Now, don't take that as another cute statement. You have to meditate on the truth of this statement; nothing that you can experience with the five senses can be a reality without the mind. If your mind didn't exist, to you, at that point, nothing exists. Existence is based on the mind because without the mind nothing can exist, thusly nothing can be experienced. As you move through life from moment to moment, your mind is constantly defining. Your mind is defining colors, shapes, measurements and extended perceptions thereof. Nothing can be to you anything without your mind. The power that your mind takes, whether it's done consciously or unconsciously, is the power to define. Nothing has color unless you say so. Nothing has shape unless you say so. Nothing has sound unless you say so. Nothing has taste unless you say so. Nothing has feeling unless you say so.

Check this out.

Things in life are not present to you; things in life are presented from you. Right now, even though you might not understand, I will say, this means everything. You will be surprised how much control over life you actually have. Things just don't happen to you, they happen from you. The reason why most people in the world do not want to believe this is because it forces responsibility. This is due to a lazy mind. A good number of people carry a "woe is me" attitude. Everything to them happens beyond their control. But the truth is, they control everything that happens to them. We are the true makers of our destiny, good or bad. Responsibility is vital. Or may I say "Your Ability to Respond" is vital.

Things just don't happen to you, they happen from you.

To help bring a clearer understanding, let's investigate from this angle and start with something that is clearly evident. Everything that you see outside of nature, meaning everything created by mankind is just that, created. There is nothing that you see in life that did not begin in someone's mind.

Name the first 10 things you immediately see around you. Nothing came into physical existence without first entering into someone's mind. This is why I said, it is important not to dismiss your desires. These are the little "things" that pop into your mind, becomes a physical reality in your body first in the form of hormone response which is still a "mind" state, and then become the physical "things" that we experience on the outside. This is proof that nothing happens without the mind.

Nothing happens without the mind.

Now you can take this same mind and determine what things are going to be by giving things purposeful definition. In order to have anything in life, you must first define those things. You do it anyway. This is much different than decision-making. You don't decide what you have for breakfast, you define what you have for breakfast, then you decide by eating the breakfast. See how much control you actually have?

People generally don't know or realize that the same power that they have over their breakfast; they also have over everything in their life. This is where the word "responsibility" comes in or as I put it, your "ability to respond". When you want something in life to happen, you have to define it first. You cannot expect things to arbitrarily happen to you. If something happens to you that you don't quite like, take responsibility by saying, "that came from me", and then redefine what you really would like to happen.

A good practice in defining is writing things down. This way you can take measurement of the results. Because everything might not turn out the way you want, and you must have your definitions written down to check the results against your original definitions. You can even do this within your relationships. The truth is, all results are based on your definitions, and it's just that sometimes your definitions are a buried subconscious belief system. Actually, everything does turn out they way you design it whether you are conscious of that design or not. But in documenting your definition, you would then have a way of knowing the difference between what you wrote on paper and the deeply laid patterns of definition buried in your subconscious. Writing things down and checking results against what's written down gives you a picture of what's on your mind.

Defining is writing things down.

Can you believe it!!!???

People actually live from day to day without having a clue as to what's on their mind. When you pay attention to your experiences outside of your mind, this is the biggest mirror of what's on your mind consciously and what's in your mind subconsciously. Here you can take responsibility or respond to your ability with clarity. You always have that choice. Define and redefine. In order to deal with those nagging things that you experience, that you don't like, or even the things you would like to make happen, but the results do not turn out quite the way you like them, you have to design what is defined.

Design the Defined

This is the basis of quality. It is also a special privilege given to mankind. I really love the root of the word design - sign. It means, "to mark". In this case you would be marking your future appointments with people, places, and things that are provided for you in order to reach your destiny based on your desires. You can picture this as developing a road map of habits. Putting up signs within your mind for direction does this for you. Deep-rooted direction. Direction and design are primarily the same action. All things that are defined need a design. Design is when you take the measuring tools and instruments of finality and bring your desire beyond the definition of what you want. Design is defining your definition and refining your definition. It's realizing direction and mapping it. This process is very important because it gives you "reference points" as you progress in your endeavors. "Reference Points" here are vital because they actually come from a master design. Having "marked points" keep you from being disappointed, and in life you are either appointed or disappointed. Without "reference points", the likelyhood of disappointment is greater. Whenever you are disappointed, it simply means that you are missing mapped out "reference points".

This is where design becomes paramount. Every thought comes with a master design that accompanies that thought. The Universe accommodates every thought and sets provision for every thought.

Let me just not say that and leave it for esoteric guessing. Remember the statement about your body being the first response to your "thoughts" as your body becomes a hormone-based reality of the mind? As far as science can reach into the Universe, it is an unequivocal fact that every element of the Universe scientifically has a mirrored existence in your body, from timed processes, mineral elements, and movements. Thought precedes any physical existence, so your thoughts move the timing of bodily functions and Universal processes. Not the other way around.

This is a part of the master design. You must prepare yourself to meet these master accommodations or "points" in your life. The best way to do this is to one, know that they exist, and secondly, map out their existence-points by designing a reference map within your mind that lead to these master accommodations.

It is more important to change the chemicals in your body than it is to try to change your mind. Here's how it works.

Emotions

First, you must get the chemicals in your body to respond to your design. Next, you must set the emotional content within your body to agree with your total wealth which already exists.

It is proven that your body reacts emotionally to every thought that you have, just like the Universe does. Emotions are key to road mapping "reference points" according to your defined desire. But you must have a clearer understanding of the construct of your emotional system in order to make this work for you. Mastering your emotional system is key to developing an affective design.

Mastering your emotional system is key to developing an affective design.

Emotions are not feelings. You experience emotion as feelings. Emotions are simply chemical constructs within your body that causes you to feel a certain way that will eventually become a catalyst to your motions or real movements in life. Emotions are signals. At the root of the word design is "sign" or in this case "assign", which is your ability to set up signals within your body that determine direction and subsequent movement in particular directions.

To make this very simple, we as humans either respond to our emotions or we set our emotions so life can respond to us. Life can respond to what you desire and define. Generally, emotions that you respond to are set by external factors. Emotions that are set by purpose-ful design are set by internal factors which match your defined thoughts and should not be set by outside influences. Design here becomes the work of both you and the Universe. This is where a great partnership can be realized. But first let me give you a simple history on your emotional make-up.

Every cell in your body is designed to agree with your success and to promote your success, literally. As I said earlier, an emotion is simply a chemical make-up or a chemical set within your body. It is an *"organized"* set of chemicals that affect the protein strands that pierce through your body's cells. Every protein strand has a receptor and these receptors collect data from the environment that give each cell its instructions to live. Here you must understand that every cell in your body holds a total picture of your entirety and based on the instructions given to these protein strands from the environment, the cells in your body form communities of cells that carry out various activities and functions for life. These communities over evolutionary time came out to be your heart community of cells, your lung community of cells, your liver community of cells, so forth and so on. And thusly your whole body and its cell communities function together as a united provision for life here on Earth. Over time, your total makeup came to be based on instructions given to these cells which are received from the environment via the protein strands with receptors on the ends. Everything in life is based on this process.

Now the key word here is environment. Everything that is biological in nature is a result of cell divide. Cell divide becomes necessary when the structure of the cell has a need to continue to evolve. It is safe to say that the very nature of cell divide is based on desire, the desire for life and the desire for more life. And over billions of years as these protein strands received information from the environment, it has forced cell divides and the re-communication of these cells to form some of the most amazing biological organisms and systems, which includes you and I. All of this is based on the chemicals that attach themselves to these receptors on the protein strand that send instructions and direction to the cell, then the cell divides and creates more of what it is. You are being pushed to create more of who you are! This is the basis of design. These chemicals are a result of what the brain processes via the environment of thought and is also what gives us the resulting emotions. These emotions then become the basis for construction and development. Let your cells within your body work for you and your vision.

Now there is something great that must be noted here. Up until about 6000-7000 years ago the design of these organisms was set by the environment and was designed to respond to the environment only. Even mankind was environment-activated based on the chemicals that attached themselves to the protein receptors that influenced cell direction. All of this was based on the environment and its influence.

Now It's You, Not Your Emotions

Something amazing happened at this point in the history of man's biological development. Divine Intelligence injected itself into mankind. Man was no longer a slave to his emotional make-up for survival. Being an exact replica now of the Divine Intelligence, man could now dictate to his emotional system by design and on purpose. These same chemical structures called emotions can now work in reverse as a system of instruction to command the environment, verses the older system where the environment commanded the structures that made up the man. Man was now set up to duplicate himself by developing the environment around him based on the desires set and organized within him. It was at this point in history that the first cities were developed, and the sciences and the arts were introduced. Having the environment to follow your instructions, the environment now under your control answers the desires within you by its availability to be structured to provide for your enjoyment. In other words, instead of "things" evolving you, you by design evolve things.

Instead of "things" evolving you, you by design evolve things.

With things in the environment having the same structures that are found in the human body which was developed over the eons of time, the environment like the cell-structures in your body and its resulting cell communities has to follow your emotional content which can be set by your design. This is how you build these "reference points" both in your body and in your environment around you.

Wow! The environment follows your emotional content!

In essence, man has a need to be loved by himself, so everything around him must conform to his make-up for him to experience his own love. There is no other basis for experiencing love. Getting what you like. Getting what you desire. Getting who and what you are presented back to you is the basis for true love.

This is why design is vital. The first thing you design is your emotional content and your environment must be checked against the content of your design. This has a great impact on how you feel in the end. You must master your emotions. Being able to master your emotions makes you a master of the Universe. This physiological system is designed to perpetuate completeness.

**Being able to master your emotions
makes you a master of the Universe.**

Relationship by Design

Relationship is paramount to your existence. In this light, every relationship that you have or form, is just as important as a marriage. Just because the government recognizes marriages officially on paper doesn't make your other relationships of any less value. Know that all information becomes formation. This is why relationships are vital to the development of anything. This counts for all of your relationships. The first presence in your personal evolution that should extend outside of yourself should be similar and simulated to you. Agreement here is vital. Then everything else in your environment must "conform" to what is "informed" in you based on your personal need or desire. In Christian text, this is called "the garden". What type of garden do you plant for yourself? What type of people do you associate with? Does it agree with or match your desire?

Let's go back to what I mentioned earlier. A major component of design is a system of "reference points". And you have to "appoint" the people, places, and things in your design. You have to set up sign structures that lead to what has been assigned as your reference points that are specific places of definition. Without definition you cannot set up these signs to the points and places of your definition. People, places, and things must match your destination. Like a GPS, you cannot assign directions without a defined place of destination. To emphasize the point, you must define the people, places, and things in your life according to your defined desire. But most of all, along with that, you must define and design your emotions and your emotional content, as this becomes a driving force to your personal development. Again, you must get the chemicals in your body to respond to your design. People you choose in life should be the first "right" responses to your dreams and desires.

Structures of Emotions

Now I want to help you with the structure of your emotions. But first, you must understand the historical structure of your emotional system. For a moment, I would like for you to understand the emotional system and its resulting cell structures within you as a tree. When I say a tree, I'm speaking in the same sense as a family tree. When tracing the genealogy of the emotional system throughout evolutionary history, as the cell divides, then reunite with other cells, they birth new cell structures. And as these cells build biological structures over time, you can map out this process from the beginning of the first single cell organism to your current human body, then a tree is formed, much like a family tree. You and I are the final form of the most complex aggregation of cell structures at the far end of this evolutionary tree. This includes the single cell to the more advanced life forms which are all making up this evolutionary tree.

Throughout the history of this tree, there is a protein strand that is the single most mitigating factor in cell direction and cell choice. The protein strand is a strand or string that pierces every cell in your body. Each strand has a receptor on its end that bond with the chemicals in your body. The emotions have always been the driving chemical system that bonds with this protein receptor. Your emotions literally have vibratory properties by nature and are in an actual and constant state of movement in your body. This movement determines the movement and activity of the protein strand, which then in turn directs the cells in your body. The environment throughout evolutionary history propelled all of this. Now don't let me lose you here. So, I will simplify this even more.

The Most Important Story Ever Told

There's a story that appears at the beginning of a number of religious texts concerning the fall of man. The story provides three elements; the persons (in this case Adam and Eve), the tree, and a snake. In this story, the snake is responsible for convincing them to take a bite of the forbidden fruit. It was said that in eating the fruit, they would be like their Creator. What was not recognized here was this; based on an earlier valuation of their Creator, they both were already made in the image of Divine Intelligence, therefore they had to reduce their personal evaluation of themselves in order to accept the instructions and redirection of the snake. The snake in the tree. The snake's job here was to point out to Adam and Eve that they were not enough. How do you get the feeling that says, "you are not enough"? The snake tells you. The snake here is not an independent force as most would think. The snake here is controlled by the emotions.

What makes this story so important? We can use this story as the perfect allegory to map out exactly how the emotions work in the body.

So now, let's take the tree again and the emotional cell make-ups throughout history that form the tree. Since the protein strand is structured just like a snake's body, we will say that the protein strands are snakes in the tree, snakes that permeate the cell body. These protein snakes throughout history are the body of information influenced by the emotion that was in turn influenced by the environment, thusly directing the construction of the tree. You are the final product of this tree, the fruit. Now it's your job to produce more fruit and not devour your own potential. You and your body are designed to produce more of what it is. But something in the tree keeps telling you, "You're not enough!".

You and your body are designed to produce more of what it is.

What becomes a point of struggle for many of us is that we are not designed to produce anything different from ourselves. A lemon tree produces lemons, an orange tree produces oranges, and an apple tree produces apples. You as an extension of the tree that extends throughout Earth's history; and as a virtual tree yourself, you contain your own system of branches complete with its own set of cells and proteins. You are literally made to produce more of who you are. You are made to multiply your very existence. Therefore, self-love is self-awareness, and self-awareness gives you the basis to reproduce and multiply yourself.

Now the protein strand as a snake that extends through the cell body is constantly providing direction. But the tendency is to draw this information and direction from environmental factors telling you that you are not enough and not your internal design. This type of environmentally controlled direction is sufficient for basic survival skills ie. eating, walking, talking etc., but the signal received by these protein receptors or snakes does emanate from the environment and allows for these basic survival skills, but not skills for building, construction skills, or the skills of imagination, creation, and development. The "snake" should not rule.

Again, once the Divine Intelligence entered into the structure of human existence, these same protein strands (snakes) and its receptors via chemical bonds can now receive instructions from your body/mind and not just the environment. The snake or protein strand no longer hold power, your mind does. We are now privileged with the gift to design, plan, map out, and direct. This is a major turn and transformation in the system! The environment is no longer the director, you are! Anytime you have the tendency to follow your primal emotions, you are listening to the snake in the tree and not your creative mind. The emotions are then powered by your environment and not by your design. You have to switch that order! Remember, you can set your "reference points".

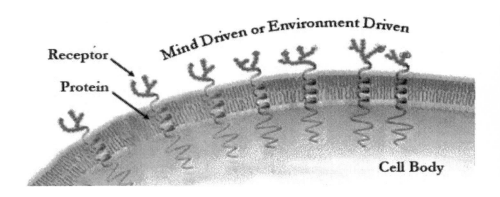

If you keep responding to your environment by means of the snake, you are not answering what's in you. You can tell that this is the case when you are left with a sense of non-accomplishment, a sense that you went in a non-optimal direction, a sense of "you need to do better", or a nagging sense of guilt. You then feel that you haven't moved forward, and you are left with a sense of incompletion. You also feel that you are repeating the same things over and over again. You feel the absences in your body.

Dealing With Your Absences

The protein strand or the snake that permeates the cell body is aware of things in the environment and the things within itself that complements the environment, which is simply anything outside of your mind that is presented to you. It then points out your absences. It is this awareness of the absences in its current body make-up that enables itself fully to deal with the surrounding environment and what it thinks it needs. Absences – "I'm not enough".

I will call these absences "shame" - the syndrome of "I'm missing something and it's embarrassing". As the environment exposes these absences within the body it becomes a signal or a sign, and with this sign via the protein strand or snake, information is passed to the cell to form or do whatever is necessary to deal with the environmental concerns by developing and directing based on signals from the environment. This design though is based on the knowledge of what might be good and the absence of good, the environment, which then determines what's needed for survival. Here your emotion is the leader, taking its cues from your environment or the current conditions around you. This is a job of the emotion and the snake that permeates the cell body, and again this is used for basic survival skills. But it is your job to forget your environment and build emotional content based on your desires.

You need to determine your design based on the good within you only and not your shame or what you think is missing. Do this in disregard to the snake in your biological tree, in disregard to your emotional make-up, and your feelings when it is negative and unproductive. Negativity flows from the sensation of the absences felt within you. A true mind bypasses all outer sensations of what might be good and the absence of good based on external factors and will focus only on the good that comes from designing and appointing. Use your body/mind! This creation comes by design from within. This keeps our continued evolvement on the desired path.

Let me skip to the point. Don't live from your absences!

When you think less of who you are, you are left only with the ability to survive based on environmental concerns and outside forces. This is mainly based on what people have to say, the neighborhood you grew up in, whether or not you have good parents, whether you've been naughty or nice, the grades you made in school, the state of the economy, whether it's raining or not, or you just broke up with your girlfriend or boyfriend, etc., etc., etc.

The events and situations that control you, make you!

When your emotion is the leader, the emotional body via the snake (protein strand) will always point out your deficiencies and perceived absences, you then work from that basis to survive.

It is hard to design properly when you are exposed to your absences or shame, because then your make-up begins to match those absences, thusly as your chemical body registers these deficiencies, you feel bad and dis-ease sets in. Your emotions then give instructions to your cells and disease follows while discomfort is then registered in your body. These same signals then register in your personal environment, and your outer environment will respond by providing more of the same content outside of yourself to match what's registering within you. The negative will keep being reproduced because your environment is designed to accord itself with your emotion. The cycle then can become habitual. Some people even go back to the source of that bad feeling again and again, thinking and believing that things are going to change, which within itself becomes a habit and a survival technique, the belief in random change, or one day someone who is hurting you will change.

This is why bad situations present themselves. Your emotions create your environment as well. What you would want to change is your emotional content by making intelligent choices based on predetermined "reference points". Design from the mind is the basis in which you direct yourself on another level outside of the influence of the snake or the protein strand. You influence the emotion.

How do you change the emotion? When you change the emotion, you actually change the chemicals that attach to the snake or the protein strands which influences your body.

At times you choose the people, the places, and the things in your life based on your shame and not your design. When you choose based on your shame or what you think is missing, you are eating the fruit from your environmental tree. When you choose based on your design, you are eating the fruit of your personal design. Both will produce more fruit after its kind.

Which direction will you choose? Check the people in your life, make sure you are not relating to them in order to resolve your shame. It will only produce more shame. The same goes for the places and things in your life. The problem in life is not that you are experiencing problems, but that you are not experiencing the good that potentially comes from your personal design. When you are not relating to your good, you are relating to people, places, and things that matches your shame, which produces more negative events.

Don't focus on your environment which will tend to tell you that you are not enough. You set the signs, draw the map, and determine the design, and then your body will develop a chemical set that will correspond to your thinking, forcing a more healthy system, because you are now giving your protein strands or the snake instruction and direction, and not the opposite.

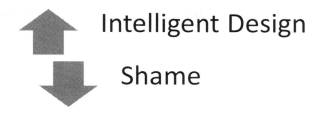

Intelligent Design

Shame

The Cell Body Is Designed to Assist Your Success

First, document your needs and then make appointments accordingly. Stick to these appointments, even when you don't feel like it. Sticking to these appointments will work up a different chemical set in your body. Then construct a map and set up the road signs. When you are feeling good about this, the chemicals within your body are now responding to your design. Now lock it in by making a determination.

Determine Your Design

Determine an endpoint to your Design. Never keep your ideas and wants open-ended. Terminate what doesn't work for you.

Determination and definition are related word concepts. The root word of determine is "termine" which means to terminate. The root word for define is finite, which is the same as making things final or bringing things to an end. How is this important to your personal development?

Once you have a design established, that design must have an endpoint established in your mind so you can have a beginning point to work with outside of your mind. Every flight of a commercial airliner has a flight plan and a determined destination for landing. What if you booked a flight that was open-ended? It would never work. It's quite simple, finishing something is important. Reaching a destination is vital once you start the journey.

Determination is the process of placing final points to your design. You need these final points not just for yourself, but you need them for others who might play a role in getting you to your destination. Have you ever thought for a little why airport terminals are called terminals? Termination is related to your destination. Everyone from the flight crew, to the ground crew, to air traffic control all have the same determination to coordinate a flight, guiding the flight to its destination. This is vital, because with anyone of these entities being off by any measure, this can spell disaster for the traveler.

Agreement

The same holds true for the design in your mind based off of your desire. It was discussed earlier the importance of the "Mind". Everything you see in existence outside of nature started in someone's mind. With this being a fact, one might conclude that the mind is the most vital component of human existence. But there is one component of human existence that stands even greater than the human mind. That component is agreement. Without agreement nothing within the mind can function outside of the mind. Agreement is the single most important word in human history. Here's where the word termination or determination becomes vital to the process of your personal success.

Everything in existence has at its base, energy. If it contains protons, neutrons, and electrons, it is governed by energy. To determine what something is going to be, you must set its energy. Energy is measured in hertz and every animate and inanimate object can be measured in hertz. Hertz is quite frequently referred to as frequency or wave patterns, and how frequencies interact determines what a substance is. To simplify what frequencies are, we can define them as wave patterns or rhythm. Any substance that exist is simply a complex interaction of rhythms. So, to determine what a "thing" is to be, you must pinpoint a basis to establish the energy needed to bring some "thing" into reality or to a finite point.

To determine what something is going to be, you must set its energy.

The mind can define and design based on a desire, but it cannot set energy. It can't do it, period. Energy is set by agreement. Agreement is a determination on how things work together in order for other things to exist. But here's that word again. Determination. Why?

What's fundamental to agreement is termination. This concept might seem strange, but its how things are. We actually make determinations by the process of elimination.

What?

The Process of Elimination By Termination

You are in a constant state of relationship. You are in a constant state of exchange. You are in a constant state of becoming one. All of these are true by default. Everything on earth, in order for it to exist has to be in relationship to something. Even the breath that you breathe is in a relationship. If it didn't work right, you would cease to exist. Relationships always foster energy in one form or the other. One of the best examples of this is photosynthesis. All organisms require energy for their chemical reactions. These reactions are involved with reproduction, growth, and other activities.

Every cell in your body is in a constant state of relationship. It is the nature of these relationships that form the basis of life and existence. What happens when one component of a stated relationship ceases to cooperate? Dysfunction would set in and the organism, whatever it may be, will begin to move towards decay and eventually death. This is true for a microorganism such as a simple cell structure or a macro-organism such as an airport, corporation, or even a government.

Organisms found in nature and in your body have set contingencies for just this matter. Whenever any part of the whole ceases to function, it is terminated. This must be so or the whole organism will follow the direction of the dysfunctional part into decay and death. Even in the organism called a corporation, when an employee is of no use to the goal of the whole, he or she is dismissed. If it is determined that a pilot is not competent to get you to your destination, it is prudent that action is taken, and the pilot is terminated from the process.

May I state a fact that is not readily recognized?

Thank you.

Every human on Earth, being in a constant state of relationship is also always in a full state of interactivity and intimacy at all times. What I mean by this is that every human on Earth is fully connected. This is a part of your complete existence, being fully connected at all times. The question then is not of connectivity, but whom and what one is connected to. Connection determines energy and energy determines state.

Connection determines energy and energy determines state.

If something bad or less desirable happens to a person, it is not because they are missing a connection, it is because they are connected to some source that creates that situation. Again, it is important to realize that at all times you are fully connected. If something bad happens, that "bad" has a source, and at some point and time you came into agreement with that source that created the energy field for that very situation to come into existence.

You are in a constant state of agreement with something and someone at all times. The state of connection never changes, only the type of connection changes, and then the resulting energy changes with it. Energy is time.

Agreement sets energy, and only through two or more sources working in proximity can energy be produced. Why is this important? Just like in nature and within a successful corporation, you have to become proficient in terminating things that don't work. A relationship to something or someone who doesn't actively agree with your destination will always produce bad results. Why? Because a relationship of any kind is still an agreement, and active agreements set the energy that facilitates form, whether that form ends up being good for you or bad for you.

Sometimes we stick with bad agreements and then try to work them out. That's why I tell people don't try to solve problems, because solving an issue brings you into a relationship to that issue, which then creates the problem. The key here is to see more than what you might consider to be the problem that is registering in your presence, because more always exist. Then relate to the more. If something bad presents itself, there is definitely something that's in disagreement with your design. Something or someone is out of line with your appointments. Signs on your roadmap are being disregarded. Whatever it is, once identified, it must be terminated. This is how real and true determinations are made. Don't become a problem solver, become an idea generator. Then get rid of what doesn't work.

Don't become a problem solver, become an idea generator.

Remember here, we are simply directing the energy into what is to be formed to reach a specific destination. It is here that we make our adjustments and to make sure that all stay in alignment with our stated goals. When you change the energy, you redirect the destiny. If the person fueling an airplane headed to California from Florida misses his cue based on assigned directives, that flight would be cut short of its destination because the line of wrong energy was not addressed and terminated.

After creation is completed in the mind and the design is set based on that creation, relationships are then fostered to address the creation that promotes those initial energy streams that eventually bring the form of that design into reality. When you have a point of destination set and a non-profitable agreement has pulled you off course, you have to terminate the wrong direction thusly setting you back on the right path.

When you change the energy, you redirect the destiny.

Changing Degrees

Here's a clearer example. When somebody disappoints you, they actually didn't. You put yourself in a line of agreement with that person, which then led to the disappointment. What you must do is terminate that direction or person, because no matter how much you try to push, your destination will never be reached. It's important to note here that all the responsibility falls on you, because you are the master designer. You can require another person to make an adjustment to accommodate your dream, but if they can't make the adjustment, you must make the termination, which then becomes your determination.

Let's use an airline flight again as an example. When a flight is headed in the wrong direction and the pilot is made aware that he or she is off course, and when the adjustments are being made to get back on course you might think of it as being just that - getting back on course. But something greater is happening here. As the pilot is adjusting the plane to what is considered to be the right course, he or she is also simultaneously terminating all possible undesired courses. As the dial on the plane's compass is rotating around to the desired mark, all other marks on the compass are being refused. Why is this important?

Really, the pilot can stop at any one of those marks on the compass. But if the pilot stops three degrees short of the desired setting, reaching the destiny will be impossible, so the three-degree mark must be terminated and refused. If the pilot stops two degrees short of the desired setting, reaching the destiny will not be possible, so the two-degree mark must be terminated and refused. If the pilot stops even one degree short of the desired setting, reaching the destiny will be impossible, so the one-degree mark must be terminated and refused. Every degree stopped on outside of the one taking the flight to its desired destination is considered to be a relationship to that degree or mark, and the energy resulting from that relationship will form another point outside of the desired destination. Time is then wasted entertaining and entraining what doesn't work.

If you are waiting for someone to change to accommodate your dream, you are stuck on that degree point. The good thing here as you terminate all the wrong degree points, you are automatically moving towards the right one. Here determination is based on what you decide to stop doing.

The soul of determination is about making cuts and letting go. It's about terminating people, places, and things that do not line up with the efforts of your destination and putting aside what doesn't work for you. I must admit, when I called myself being on the diet that I had determined, so I thought, I was going to eat all the right foods, and I did. But as a part of the process, I never stopped eating the bad foods and my destination remained distant. Even when I had a super exercise session, I would celebrate with a bowl of ice cream.

For many people, with all the effort that is made to reach a destination, their destination remains distant. They were determined to reach their goal. They did all the right things. True. It is a great thing to set goals and map out a course of action. They did all the required steps to reach their destination. But here's the issue, they "started doing" without the "stop doing" that was necessary to make a true determination. If you feel stuck, or if you are stuck, then it's a 99.99% chance that this is at the root of your being stuck. Remember, the soul of determination is about making cuts and letting go.

Decide What's Determined

Decisions are a matter of intimacy.

A friend of mine who is a renowned psychologist used to always state this poignant analogy. It goes as follows: There are three frogs on a log, one decided to jump off, how many frogs are left on the log? Many knowing that this was a trick question were hesitant in stating the obvious "two" that would be left. People would wrestle with the answer for a while to pinpoint the source of the trick in the question. But after a short time, they would resolve to the answer, "two". My friend would say in response, "wrong answer". People then would begin to insist that if three frogs were on a log and one decided to jump off, invariably two would be left. This went on for a period of time before my friend would reveal the shocking answer, "If there were three frogs on the log and one decided to jump off, there would be three frogs remaining on the log."

What?!!!?

What was the great wisdom behind the trick of all trick questions?

Here it is. The answer was that there were three frogs left on the log because one only decided to jump off, but never did.

Movement is not mental, it is actual. The key element to decision making is movement. This is why I stated earlier that a decision is a matter of intimacy. It is about closeness and being close. Moving in close.

Does this make sense? I want you to consider here that every decision you make is about entering into a relationship. For anything to be done in life, a relationship has to be a prerequisite to that accomplishment. We generally do not pay attention to the fact of what I mentioned earlier that every "thing" in life is in a constant state of relationship. It takes relationship to make a true decision. This is why it is vital in life to determine who and what you are close to. You must be active in documenting your relationships for review, especially if you are in a situation where you are not progressing.

It takes relationship to make a true decision.

If you decided to make a certain move in life or to take a specific action, that decision is not really made until an action is completed. You need to pay more attention to completed actions versus mental intentions, both in what you decide, and more importantly in what people decide towards you.

A person that lives in Florida who has made a trip to California and calls you, saying "I'm in California, I have decided to take a trip to California", holds greater validation and value than a person residing in Florida and while in Florida tells you, "I have decided to take a trip to California." Both stated a decision that was made. But only the person who is actually in California has made a definitive decision. Only the decisions acted on are true decisions. That's why all decisions are a point of intimacy.

Only the decisions acted on are true decisions.

When you have a mate that you love and you want that person to fully realize that they are loved, you have to decide to take actions that show love. The worse thing that you can do is to declare love without performing actions. You have decided to be with that person, but that person has no experience extended from you to realize any love. This is when it's usually said, "You're all talk". How can a person experience your love without your touch, or you at some point making a purchase of something that they can see and hold, or cooking a nice meal that they can taste? Get the point?

You should also expect active decisions towards yourself, destiny, and desired accomplishments. A person speaking towards you without the actions declaring the same value of the language spoken, is of little value. They are all talk. How can you experience love without the decision including some type of action?

The same goes for every decision you make in life. A lot of people make decisions, but it only happens within their head. When you encounter such a person, you will also encounter a trail of things left undone, promises broken, with no measurable follow-through. That's because intimacy was left out of the formula. Decisions are steeped in connection. Decision-points should be connecting-points. You have to connect to what you are going for. Intimacy.

How do you get what's in your head, out of your head? Remember it's about intimacy. Every great idea in your head, in order for it to come out of your head, must prepare itself for some type of relationship to begin its journey to becoming realized. You first must create an environment conducive for those ideas to survive outside of your head. Why do I say survive? Because any idea that attaches itself to a non-substantive relationship will die.

Look at it this way.

We live in a polarized environment called Earth. Everything on Earth either lives or dies, it's up or down, it goes backwards or forward, it is either in or out. Direction is intricate to existence on earth and in the Universe. All direction is determined by you and determined by what you decide.

So, you say, "I want to do this...". Well what does it take to get this...done?

Good relationships and agreement. Intimacy.

Determination is about planting a garden for your good ideas by getting rid of all the weeds. Also, by making sure the soil is conducive for proper growth and keeping predators at bay. Again, it's about terminating anything that doesn't work. This is pivotal to decision making.

You really can get excited now about accomplishing your goals, because every idea that hits your mind is a guarantee that that idea is already accomplished. The beginning of every "thing" always starts in the mind. When an idea comes to your mind, get excited! It has begun. The idea, by beginning in your mind validates its own existence. The fact that you can "think it" extends you past the point of "creating it". It is here. What you want is here!

A point that is vital to understand, is that everything needed to relate to what's in your mind and to bring it into reality is already here in reality. Now I am going to move a step beyond what most religious, personal development, and motivational experts teach you at this point. That is the notion of "now you have to just believe it". Most people have trouble doing that. They say at this point it is a matter of faith. What I'm going to do is change that for you, because belief and faith is currently understood to be a mental matter and I'm going to make belief and faith a point of physical matter and then making a decision.

Evidence

Write this down. Look for evidence. Do not have faith. Do not believe.

Do not believe in your dreams; do not have faith that you can accomplish what you want in life!

What?!!??

Look for evidence. Why? Why disregard the traditional understanding of belief and faith?

When something hits your mind as a great idea, which then metastasizes into a desire, the only basis of it coming to your mind is that it exists already, but not just in your mind. It also exists outside of your mind as a physical reality. This is not a statement of belief as we know it! This is not a statement of faith as we know it! It actually is. This is where our traditional understanding of belief and faith becomes irrelevant.

What?!!?

Yes, the physical reality of everything that you have in your mind actually exists. The key here is to begin to experience what already exist. Move towards experience as the evidence presents itself. Again, this is not a faith effort, nor is it a belief effort. Now, for the Christian, I must tackle the word "faith" to destroy these erroneous notions.

The Christian Bible says, "That faith is the substance...".

So, let's stop here.

Faith is a substance. Faith has the quality of being substantial and it is something that exists in physical reality. Faith is the physical matter in which you use to develop what is pictured mentally. When things don't happen in your life, it simply means that you are relating to the wrong substances which are needed to bring about your desire. That's why I say that the decision-points in your life are a matter of intimacy and connection, because the subsequent relationships determine your faith or results, which then become your faith - things that actually exist.

Faith is also the "evidence" of things not seen. What is not seen is the idea in your mind. Your desire. Now ask yourself, what is outside of you that is the evidence of what's inside you? Remember, the key to spirit is moving from what can't be seen, to moving to what can be seen. Your mind has to be redirected. When you look at the "seen", the stuff that makes up this world, what do you see? More importantly what do you see that relates to what is planted in your mind?

The problem here is when we have a great idea, we do not look for the evidence of that great idea within the things in which we see, taste, touch, smell, and hear, leaving us to relate to existences that has nothing to do with what's in our mind. People then try to use the "Christian" version and understanding of faith to make things happen.

"Just believe and you will receive".

"Just have faith".

Or the latest motivational "rah rah" statements,

"Believe it and you will achieve it".

"You can do it, yes you can".

Before you decide to move on anything, look for the evidence of it being in agreement to what's planted in your mind. We should be masters of what's in our mind and masters of coming into right agreement with what's outside of our mind. The "things" outside the mind is the substance of the "things" inside the mind. When you make a decision, to whom and to what then are you relating to? That is your faith. Faith is the substance... Faith is what you relate to that mirrors your desire.

We should be masters of what's in our mind and masters of coming into right agreement with what's outside of our mind.

First, you must master opening your eyes to those things that match and agree with what's in your mind. Secondly, when it is right, then you have to make an active decision to get involved with that "thing" or persons. All other options and involvement must be terminated. Why? Any other involvement outside of what is desired, defined, designed and determined is a distraction away from "what is" — that is the substance provided for your success. And I define distraction as "dis-action" or distance from relative action. This is the action you take that is related to what's on and in your mind, intimate relative action.

It's Here

Let's do the math to further prove the point. You have an idea to build a great building. You have a vivid picture of what that building is to be. First of all, all the materials for that building exist. This is a physical reality. Faith is a physical reality!

Secondly, there's steel available for the framework, there's wood available for the trusses, there's sand available for the concrete, there's another type of sand available for the glass, there's knowledge available for the engineering, there's knowledge available for the assembly of components etc, etc. If you add these existences to the vivid picture in your mind, then the whole of the building actually exists in its entirety immediately. After the recognition of these facts, then the only event that has to happen now is the arrangement of the physical components that coordinates with your mental component.

Since the earth is full of these materials and knowledge, then every thought that is pictured would only be the beginning of what is already in existence waiting for arrangement. Have you decided to make these arrangements or are you still sitting on the log? You have the power to arrange your friends, mentors, business partners, and lovers along with physical materials to achieve any desire.

It is here wherein you make the people, places, and things match your design or you fire them! All ends have to match your ends, or you will never reach an end. You will end up in "La La" land if they don't line up. Deciding is active acts that create memories that reflect back to your design. This is what gives us a sense of closeness. Intimacy. Without memory there is no closeness to the design that happens in the mind. Don't plan your life, create the memories that unfold.

All ends have to match your ends or
you will never reach an end.

Memory here is vital. What type of memories are you feeding back to your mind? Does it match your design? If it doesn't, you have to restructure the relationships to create a new memory. Your memory will actively tell you what's not arranged properly in your life. Remember, deciding what not to do is as important as deciding what to do.

Get off the log and make intimate and passionate decisions based on actions.

Develop What's Decided

Development is the construction and the arranging of structure. Development is a beautiful thing and there are four areas that make up the structure of development, which are in a state of simultaneous construction at all times; mind, emotion, motion, and monument. These four areas should be considered as one system of development. Quite naturally, there has been focus on one or the other as it concerns most personal development programs and self-help projects. But here, it is important that you view all four as a unit; the mind, the emotions, your movements, and your monuments.

Mastery of the four structures of development as a unit will guarantee your success in every venture. These four structures are key functions of memory. Let's take a closer look.

1. Mind
2. Emotion - the initial embodiment of the mind.
3. Motion - the physical relationships to the mind.
4. Monument - the physical structures that become the resting place for the mind.

All four of these are fundamental to memory, which then becomes the bases of all experience, both good and the not so good. These four areas are fully controlled by you and are never at the mercy of anybody or anything but you. Every person on the planet Earth is equally rich in all four areas but are not equally aware of the state of these four structures in their life, hence the difference between wealth and poverty. To help you to understand the value of this, I will employ a play-on-words scenario to make this concept ring through.

Minting

I would like to change the word development into develop-mint. The word "mint" is crucial to this analogy and is so serious, that you might consider it to become a part of your everyday vernacular.

The word "mint" is defined as follows: As a noun, it is a place where something is manufactured. As a verb, it means to create and produce, or to cause to attain an indicated status.

The most popular use of the word "mint" is understood as the making of money or coins. With this notion, anything that is minted becomes a basis of exchange using things that are valued and have value. In this case, what is valued? Whatever is in or on your mind. Everything that is on your mind can only become a true experience once it is developed outside of your mind. Things, in order to be things, must be minted into existence. So, development has to become stapled to your desired existence and the foundation for your life experiences.

I want to remind you of the four areas of structure: mind, emotion, motion, and monument.

1. Mind
2. Emotion - the initial embodiment of the mind.
3. Motion- the physical relationships to the mind.
4. Monument - the physical structures that become the resting place for the mind.

Now let's add in my little play on words using the word "mint" as a base.

1. Mind = Mint
2. Emotion - the initial "in-body-mint" of the mind.
3. Motion - the physical relationships to the mind or your acknowledgements "act-knowledge-mints".
4. Monument "money-mint" - the physical structures that become the resting place for the mind.

Without "things" there is no rest. Monuments (money- mints) or the "money that you mint" is staple to your ability to rest and be at peace. No this is no joke. The root of the word monument is from the Latin word "monere", which means to remind. This is the basis for memory. The root word for money "moneta" which means to mint is a derivative of "monere", which is the same as monument. Stay with me.

Without "things" there is no rest.

The prefix to all of these words is "mon-" which means the mind or to think. This is why I said, it is so important to value what you think. It is also imperative to think only thoughts that have value. As the old adage states, "A mind is a terrible thing to waste", so stop wasting your mind. Literally, wasting your mind is wasting money. More about that later.

Wasting your mind is wasting money.

We will start with monuments or "money-mints". If you can begin to see every "thing" that comes from you as monuments, you are off to a good start. The right monuments around you can provide you and your mind the "rest" and peace that it needs. You have to be able to rest in your creations. The mind and the monuments of the mind are closely associated and irrevocably tied together. The relation of both play a critical role as it concerns your memory. Why is memory here important?

Memory

Memory is the key to all life. Everything in life, meaning every existence carries memory. Even rocks carry memory. The first dynamic of memory is to "recall" or the ability to recall. The method that is used to incite recall is important. If you were to travel through an unknown territory and had a need to get back to your originating point, you would need a system in place to recall the directions back. Like the famous, early pioneers such as Daniel Boone and Lewis and Clark; they marked their trails so their way back can be easily identified. Monuments in your life are memory marks for future direction. What things are you monumenting, what people are you monumenting, what situations are you monumenting? What are you money-minting?

Memory is a fascinating concept. Your computer holds memory that is stored on a form of rock called silicon. A pigeon can fly hundreds of miles and somehow the return path is stored either in the mind of the pigeon or a flight path is mysteriously stored in the sky. The same goes for television and radio signals. The memory of the video signal that you can pick up locally on your television screen maintains itself through the air as it is consistently rebroadcasted into your home. All plant and animal life work and maintain its existence based on memory. A seed holds memory. Stored in an apple seed is not a plan for what a tree will be, but the memory of what the tree is.

Pay close attention here.

Everything in life produces based on memory and not planning. Now you know why a great deal of plans do not work out. There is no good memory. Yes, I said it. Success in life is not about creating good plans; success in life is about creating good memories. You can only birth what is remembered. You can plan all day, but if there is no system of rooted memory, you cannot produce a thing.

Success in life is about creating good memories to count on.

You all have heard of lottery winners winning millions of dollars, but within two to three years they end up broke. That's because they can only birth what is remembered. Even with literal wealth in the palm of their hands, their plan to live a good life for the rest of their life never pans out. On the other hand, let's take a millionaire who built his or her fortune from the ground up. If they lost every dime that they had, these same people can take a quarter and within the same two to three years recreate their millions. Memory.

When a basketball player is standing at the free throw line at practice, shooting two to three hundred free throws, he's not planning on being a successful free throw shooter; he's creating a memory. When a coach and his players watch thousands of hours of footage of great plays relevant to their sport, they are not drafting a plan to win; they are creating a memory of winning.

Development is about creating good memories, and within these four areas; mind, emotion, motion, and monument, you must develop a good memory set. Good memory sets create great energy sets. So now, anything that you "mint" becomes a part of your memory.

To be successful and to grow exponentially, take stock in your monuments. This is a good place to start to measure what's actually on your mind or minted in your mind.

Remember when I mentioned the garden earlier? Take stock in your garden. You have to guard your garden. What's in it? What people are in it? What things are in it? How are people and things arranged around you? Does it add continued value to your life? If not, get rid of it!

You have the right and the ability to place good monuments around you. But most importantly you have to take stock and measurement in what you create physically or "measure what you are minting" in your life - (measure-mint). Everything that you create, every relationship that you are involved in is a minted existence and your monuments become a vital part of your memory.

Building Emotions

Now, the emotions. Ninety-nine percent of the actions that you take are based on emotions, which is the in-body-mint of what's on your mind. Emotions are literal chemical sets that rest in your body. Most people are unaware of the innate need to develop and structure this particular structure along with everything else in life. Generally, this is because most people view emotions as something that happens to them. Emotions do not happen to you, they happen from you.

Just like any of the other structures, you must take responsibility for your emotions. With the emotions being such a critical part of your total make-up, you have to realize that emotions can be designed and structured just like anything else. Remember that your emotions should match the desires of your mind and not be responsive to your immediate environment. So, your emotions must be built and not influenced. This becomes a purposeful action.

Constructing your emotions can eventually become a simple thing to do, but it will take some practice. The emotions and the environment are closely tied, and this is a hard fact to get away from. You first must approach your emotions from the mind and not the environment. The emotions sit almost dead center between the two. Since you have full control over your mind and full control over your immediate environment, then it stands to be an absolute fact that you have full control over your emotions.

The chemical sets in your body known as the emotions are designed to be super sensitive and super responsive to environmental stimuli and mind stimuli. Remember at one point in our evolutionary history, it was just the environmental stimuli that effected our emotions, but now we are gifted with a powerful mind that can direct the emotions. The key here is that whatever is minted in your mind, you have to mint those same facts in your body, "in-body-mint".

Your body and its make-up are designed to become the first initial construct of what you dream about. Yes, that's what I said. If you dream about becoming a doctor, what's in your body must become a doctor first. If you want to build a great architectural structure, that structure must be built within your body first. If you want to make a million dollars, the million dollars is made in your body first. Things that become things, happen within the body first. You literally have to "mint" these things into your body. Your body is the first manufacturing plant for anything you want in life. The first things manufactured after a great idea or when a destiny is set are the chemical sets in your body called emotions.

Yes. Think of your body as a manufacturing plant. Most psychologist, self-help gurus, personal development specialist, and spiritual leaders focus on the mind structures, and rightfully so. But we miss the body structure, which is the first resulting system that stems from the mind. When things do not get manufactured in the body, it becomes literally impossible to realize any vision or goals outside of the body.

That's why you have to become an expert at minting things first within your body. Your whole body is a functional system of memory. Emotions are "in-body-mints" or things minted within the body. So again, if your goal is to become a doctor, the chemicals in your body must say the same thing. If you want to earn a million dollars, there are chemicals in your body that must say the same thing.

Many people fail to accomplish things in life because the chemicals in their body are not in agreement with their mind. This is what is happening when you set an aggressive life goal one day, and you wake up the next morning and don't feel like doing anything. That's because your mind is heading in one direction and the chemicals in your body are heading in another direction. Another way of looking at this is that your mind is playing one rhythm and the chemicals in your body are playing a completely different rhythm.

The mind and the emotions must be in sync along with your movements and your resulting monuments.

Again, the construction of your emotions is very deliberate. Your emotions need to be a decision point and not a reaction point. What are we talking about here?

> Focus.
> Choice of attention.
> Looking for and looking at the things that match you.

Finding the evidence. As I stated before, looking for evidence outside the mind that's congruent with the "things" that are on and in the mind. First you have to embody your dream so much to the point that you can sense the difference of what's not like you and what is like you. You are made to produce more of you, so knowing who you are is pivotal.

Directing Motion

To help you understand this, I must move on to the third structure, which is motion. Motions are the physical relationships to the mind. Focus is about what you decide to acknowledge in your life. Your acknowledgements become a vital force to your embodiments. This is critical. Just like your mind is a powerful tool, what you in-body is equally powerful.

I must state here as a reminder, that your chemical emotional system is not designed as a reactive system, but it is designed as a biochemical system to illuminate any outside entity that is unlike your mind and personal make-up. It also illuminates any outside entity that becomes a threat to who you are so you can react. If a cat had no sense that a dog is there to bite its neck off, it would never be able to determine to run. Emotions are designed to illuminate differences so you can make a determination as to how to act.

In many cases, people's emotions are all over the place because they allow their emotions to react to environmental stimuli; what people say or do, the weather, financial status, bad hair days etc. What you want to do here is change from a reactive system to a system that you deliberately and purposefully construct. When this is done, your emotions will become a system that will enable you to tell the difference and sense the difference of what's not like you and what's not like your goals and desires so you can then act accordingly.

With this being the case, your emotional system now becomes your greatest ally in identifying people and things that are like you that are in agreement with your dreams, visions, or goals. This also determines your actions and your movements, which is your motion. The resulting actions and the constructed emotional systems become functional memories that lead to greater achievements. How do you think a basketball player is able to make a free throw with 15,000 fans from the opposing team screaming and sending all their energy towards him to miss the shot? Memory. His emotions are in check and the opposition cannot shake him. So, his motion matches his memory and not the external stimuli. Practice.

Little memories build big dreams. So, what and whom we make our motions towards is a function of relationship and is minted into memory. It is all based on our acknowledgements or what we choose to act towards. So, I'm restructuring this word to "act-knowledge-mints". What you act on based on any knowledge, whether good or bad, becomes minted into existence and immediately becomes a function of memory. It is literally stored in your body.

Now let's approach this from the mind point of view. If you focus on something long enough, it becomes a part of you. Why do you think it's so hard for a woman to let go of a no-good boyfriend? Because he doesn't just exist only outside of her, he also exists in her body because over time he has been a point of focus. She then feels that she's letting go of a part of herself, because to a major degree, that's who she identifies with.

If she changes the frequency in her mind and hold correct thoughts long enough, the frequency in her body changes also, then the same mental focus and frequency becomes minted in her body. The boyfriend changes, even if it means that a new boyfriend has to come into the picture.

A second option is, is that she can be strong enough to make an intellectual decision and change the boyfriend to begin with. This is setting a new motion, and then the motions in her body will correct itself over time. Now, when she meets the old boyfriend, the corrected emotional body shows up and shows her the difference. She can then act accordingly when he says, "Baby I want you back." No!

When you are setting a chart for success in business or any other matter, you have to focus until the chemicals in your body changes. Your movements must match your focus. The physical monuments around you must agree with your focus.

As you can see all four structures; mind, emotion, motion, and your monuments have to be developed at the same time. Remember, to get to your goal which is your monument, to accomplish your dream which is your monument, to realize a purpose which is your monument, and to achieve success which becomes monumental, development must take place among all four structures and not just with your monuments.

So here are some tips for development.

1.   Remember that even before you accomplish any type of physical and observable development, that the same paralleled development must take place in your mind, emotions, and your motions also.

2.   Remind your mind by putting mini monuments in front of you. This can be a storyboard. You can record a video of you stating your goals. You can do the same with audio. You can also do this by writing down your ideas and visions and reading them before you go to bed and as you wake up in the morning.

3.   To align your chemical sets in your body with your mind, you must develop and structure those chemicals. Practicing can do this. Practice your success. Remember this is a decision point. In small ways, begin to be what you intend to be right now in many "mini" ways and then repeat. For example: if you want to own a restaurant someday, make your kitchen your restaurant now and practice every dish you wish to serve daily, even if they have to be little, tiny, affordable mini dishes. You can always be what you want to be now in some way shape or form. Remember, you cannot birth "what's next" without creating "what is" now. Your emotions can be that archetype in which you have full control of building now.

You cannot birth "what's next" without
creating "what is" now.

4.   As far as your motions are concerned it is important to complete any task that is unfinished. This is a vital component to memory. In your daily movements, connect with people and things that are aligned with your purpose, goals, and visions. Actively mark and measure those so you can be well aware of when they don't.

5.   Just like with the emotions, your mini monuments have to carry a sign of your greater goals and purposes. Every major retail chain or food chain started with one store and the subsequent stores were birthed out of that one. Always do the one well which will set the criteria for your monuments to become a sign to your next level of existence.

Destine What's Developed

This is driving what's in you. You are the center to all that is and the center of all that is. The sum total of "you" is the sum total of all that is. You are all that is which is fulfilling all that is. The question becomes, at what rate and how well are you doing the fulfilling?

Everybody on Earth has the same job description. That is to become everything. To realize everything. To be or not to be is not the question. "You are" is the answer. Embodied within you is the map of total existence. Experience is about growing into the selected facets and forms of that existence. A tree extending from a seed grows into what it already is and not to what it is to be. A tree can't be if it is already. In other words, a tree can't be a future reality if it is what it is as a seed. Every dream you have is a present reality because it exists in your mind as a seed, therefore it is not a future existence, but a present existence that is developing. To be or not to be is not the question when "you are" is the answer. So, let's start with that.

To be or not to be is not the question.
"You are" is the answer.

A seed.

Reproduction

Every biological form produces or reproduces after its kind. The basis of this reproduction is memory. Anything that cannot recall itself ceases to exist. This is why I am emphasizing again that "recalling" is important, but you have to have memory in order to recall. Within a seed, an orchard exists already. But that orchard does not vary from the seed. You do not plant a lemon seed and then years later have a plethora of lemon trees, apple trees, peach trees, cherry trees etc. No, just lemon trees.

Early microorganisms reproduced after its kind, but as time passed, these things began to advance as the environment pushed into these early formations new memories that brought about altered and advanced life forms that extended out from previous life forms. These advances were passed on as memories, but like the lemon tree, they were limited in its potential to diversify. "Seed" is about passing on memory, so "what's next" can be birthed to continue life.

"Seed" is about passing on memory, so "what's next" can be birthed to continue life.

As I said earlier, "mind" was added to the most complex biological "seed form" in existence, the human body. This mind came with unlimited diversification, abilities, and possibilities. Therefore, the mind does not have to wait for generations to create something new because it can control the structures of memory. A mind can observe a "bird form" which has posited itself within the evolutionary chain and say, "I would love to fly like that bird", and then begin to immediately develop ways to fly.

The technology for night vision goggles came from an owl. Sonar technology came from the whale. Some of our most ingenious water ways controlled by sophisticated dam systems came from watching beavers. Our mapping and GPS systems came from observing the stars. See how memory works. Are we learning from nature or are we remembering our own capabilities?

Destining - A Natural Process

At every point in the Earth's and the Universe's developmental history, something was driven to the next level. So, what drives us? Destiny. We as humans live in a systemic existence of conclusions. But we must know that all things are concluded already and is moving in stages towards the realization of these conclusions. Why?

The greatest chemicals that our body excretes are dopamine and serotonin - the happy drugs. Whenever something is concluded or reached that is idealized, there is a super sensation of euphoria. This euphoria is our resting place. It is the basis of all experience - "I've done it!" - finished. Triumph is at the core of all human existence. Accomplishment is who we are. Seeing what's next is what drives everything and every human being on Earth. Destiny is a function of human existence.

Triumph is at the core of all human existence.

The story of the "whole" is the story of you. You are the sum total of everything, because within you is the seed of everything, or better stated, the memory of everything. You are not tied down like the grass of the fields to a mundane existence. You are not limited like the lemon tree. You are not constricted like insects. You don't have boundaries like fish. You are not fixed to the ground like mammals. You are not confined to the sky like the stars. You are not circumscribed like the sun. The essence of who you are, whatever you decide to be, is waiting for development and then you have to destine what is developed.

Destine is a rarely used verb. It means - to set aside for a specific purpose. The Latin derivatives of destine means "to stand". This means to stand on something that is predetermined or decreed beforehand. Here every motion makes a stand based on memory. In your movements, you have to be consistent towards what's on your mind, and to do that you must also be consistent in the setting of your monuments.

You have to be consistent towards what's on your mind.

Most people don't realize how many things they do during the course of the day that has nothing to do with what they want to do. So, their movements are not based on where they take a stand, thusly their destinies are never realized. The advice here is very simple.

At every possible incremental time period, push your idea to the next level. Reach a new destination. Mark it. And then Move it.

Deal What's Destined

Dealing is the basis of value. Deal to those around you who agree with you and your development. This is the basis for expansion and growth.

Most of the prisons that inhibit you from reaching your destinations are due to the aggregation of people that you have around you. I mentioned earlier about agreement and the value of agreement when it comes to exchange, and as I have said, you are in a constant state of exchange. Knowing this, why would you exchange with persons who don't agree with you? That's bad economics.

People value exchange in every other medium except for what they value within themselves. If you paid $7.00 for a meal at McDonald's and you were handed a screwdriver, that screwdriver has nothing to do with you obtaining satisfaction. You couldn't even cook it as a substitute. It doesn't make sense. Does it? But yet we make daily exchanges with people that add no value to our destiny.

The reason why "dealing" here is so consequential is because dealing is the basis of production at all times. If anything is produced, it came from a deal. It came from some type of exchange, whether conscious or unconscious. You are constantly making a deal. The question is; are you consistently making the deals that increase your bottom line?

Every human being on Earth is pregnant at all times.

What?

Yes, you are in a constant state of producing something. You are also in a constant state of giving and receiving seeds to produce any and everything that's on your mind. Ask yourself, what and who's seed am I carrying? And more importantly, to what and to whom are you giving your seeds to for fertilization? A lot of our ideas die at the next person. A lot of who we are personally dies at the next person.

You are in a constant state of producing something.

People around you should take the energy of who you are and produce more of who you are. Let's view this from the standpoint of suicide. Generally, by the time a person is ready to commit suicide, they are already dead. They might have died many times over because of their surrounding system of personages that are dead. They have dealt out who they are consciously or unconsciously to entities, situations, and people who can't return anything of value back to them. Seeds can't grow in non-nutritional environments.

People around you should take the energy of who you are and produce more of who you are.

A lot of times people don't look for the evidence of who they want to be in the things surrounding them or in other people before they invite them into their environment. There ends up being a constant draw on our life force just by the associations we make. As I told you, memories are stored everywhere in our bodies and as we make contact and connections with others, memories are exchanged at different levels of degree. Even a simple touch or a hello activates an exchange.

I tell young women all the time, be careful with who you sleep with, because you're always getting pregnant whether you like it or not. You might not carry a literal baby away, but you can carry away depression, lack of aggressiveness, poverty, non-care and much more that's planted in your body as a seed. Check this out.

Have you ever had a simple conversation with a person and afterward you sensed that something is wrong with you? Well it is. To some degree, that person planted in you some of who they are and if you have any notion of fertileness to that implantation, you become pregnant with their issues without even knowing it. In the same light you could be having a not so good day and speak a short while with someone who carries good energy, and then for some reason, from that point on, your day is brighter and you feel optimistic. Yes. You just picked up some good babies. Either way, this principle is always at work.

There are some people that can walk in a room and kill a party just by their presence. But on the other hand, there are some people that can walk into a dead party and their very presence will light up the room and the party gets started. That's because there is a constant state of exchange and dealing in everything that's done.

You must deal with the people around you that either reflect you or reflect who you want to be. People must reflect your destination. This is the most powerful notion in existence. This is the area in life where we generally make the least adjustments but expect the greatest results. Write this phrase down for future use:

People around you must reflect your destination.

"If people don't grow with you, you have to outgrow them".

This is why marking your monuments is vital. Most people ignore the growth around them and still expect for growth to take place within them. People are monuments. Ask yourself this question, what memories are being activated within you when you are dealing with someone? What is your structured emotion telling you?

Creation is an opportunity, but there is no creation without co-creation. The mind that you have is unlimited in its potential, so subsequently the things you desire to have and the destinies that you desire to reach is unlimited. The most exciting thing is that because of your mind, all stages of development are guaranteed, and your destiny is guaranteed.

There is no creation without co-creation.

You have to stand on your destiny by engaging those people and things that align with your destiny. Mark it and move to the next level. The four structures of development; mind, emotions, motion and then monuments must be constructed together as one affects the other. You have to get what's in your mind out of your mind. Movement is not mental, but it is actual and active. Never keep your ideas and wants open-ended and terminate what doesn't work for you. This is best done when you have documented what does work for you, which is essential to your design. You arrange all of this. You are the great creator of your life. A destiny desired, a destiny defined, a destiny designed, a destiny determined, a destiny decided upon, a destiny developed, a destiny destined, and a destiny dealt to the right people is a destiny fulfilled.

After this new Desires are born.

The 4 Success Principles

Perception

One of the most important things in life is discovering who you are in the world. Becoming who you are starts with discovering who you are. This whole process of discovering who you are is initiated in the mind. Whatever is on your mind in the form of the thoughts is definitive of your total existence. Thoughts are vital to your personal definition and thoughts fall under the control of others when your thoughts are not managed specifically by you. But let's get a better understanding of total existence.

Everything is everything. What I mean by this is that everything exists within everything because everything is derived from the same base substance. If you were a scientist, you would understand that all physical things derive from protons, neutrons, and electrons, and every element in existence is just an arrangement of these three basic substances. At its core, everything is everything. Everything is the same.

Let's take one thing. Anything. And I will call it an "item".

Mathematic Proportional Arrangements

"Items" defined are mathematic proportional arrangements within everything. Think of everything as a whole and then let's take a pencil for example. This pencil is a mathematic proportional arrangement of elements that exist within the whole of everything. The reason why I use the word mathematical in this definition is because items within the whole can be measured and this measurement becomes the definition of what that item is. This pencil, for example, has weight, length, and color and this pencil also exist as an item within the whole of everything. This same pencil broken down into its basic elements is made out of the same substance as everything else in the world - protons, neutrons, and electrons.

You have a body that exists in this world of everything, which is also a mathematic proportional arrangement of protons, neutrons and electrons. But why does this body of yours exist in the world? Why do you exist in a world of things, items, and physicality? What is your purpose in the world? Why are you here? You, as a human being exist in the mist of things. Why? Even the individual components of your body make up a systemic existence of things, which exist in the whole of everything.

How is this relevant to discovering who you are in the world? How is this relevant to your purpose in life? How is this relevant to discovering who you are?

Let's start back with the pencil.

No one will ever deny that when you think of a pencil, you become immediately aware of its purpose. How does a pencil end up with purpose? A pencil is used for writing. Most people will agree that this is the general purpose of a pencil. Most things that are "items" in the world have definition based on its appearance in the world. If you see a yellow stick that has a pointed cylinder-like tip with a black point protruding, your mind will associate what you see as a device for writing.

That pencil derives its purpose by its mathematic proportional arrangement of protons, neutrons, and electrons, which gives it a specific appearance in the world. But the pencil's appearance does not make it what it is. It's how we see the pencil that gives it its definition. Perception.

Purpose Based on Perception

When I was younger, my brother and I would go to a store called Spencer's located in the mall. We would buy a bar of soap that wasn't actually soap. It was called trick soap. It was a fake bar that wouldn't lather. We then took the bar and replaced it with the real soap before my dad would take a shower. We waited by the bathroom door to get this anticipated response of terror as my dad would fervently try again and again to lather his washcloth with what was in his mind to be a bar of soap. My father would then yell out to my mother, "There's something wrong with this soap!" But because to him, the bar that he was looking at was soap, he would try to lather his washcloth again and again, but to no avail. Our stomachs would be cramped with laughter.

His intensity was based on his perception of what he was looking at. Because of its appearance, he assigned the bar its purpose, even though the bar did not perform. All items within the whole of everything derive its purpose based on perception.

"Items" are mathematic proportions and formulations within the whole of everything. But "items" derive its purpose based on perception and perception is a function of the mind. If you want to know your purpose in the world, it has to start with your perception; and perception is how you chose to experience the world and the items in it. Just like my dad perceived the soap to be soap.

Perception is how you chose to experience the world and the items in it.

But perception has an even greater power. Perception also contains the power of arrangement. Remember those mathematic proportions and formulations that define items in the world? This all comes from the arrangement of the formulations that give items its proportion, which then can be measured. All arrangements synthesize into purpose based on perception, which is then the cause of experience.

Remember as I said earlier. You are the great arranger of life. Perception is the beginning of all arrangements. You have the power to have any experience you desire in life. If you want the experience of being rich, you can. If you want the experience of being comfortable, you can. If you want the experience of being loved, you can. But you are fully responsible for all arrangements that cause these experiences.

Matter and The Mind

The world or the "whole" consist of two major proponents of existence, one is matter as we discussed earlier that is based on the arrangements of proton, neutrons and electrons, and the other is that which is not matter – the mind. Matter, which is everything that is experienced or that can be experienced, is derived from that which is not matter – the mind. Both exist. You exist in the world as that which is not matter - your mind and its perception, but you are experiencing life through that which is matter. When you can properly make arrangements in the world of that which is not yet matter, then that which is matter mirrors this arrangement and presents itself from you for experience. Matter and Non-Matter make the whole.

You are a mathematic proportional arrangement and formulation within the whole of everything also, but with the capability of deciding to what extent of everything you will be. The extent of who you are and what you are in the world is intricately tied to your perception. Perception is most powerful because it can change any experience immediately! This does not have to involve any form of religious right, spiritual incantation, meditation, or any other related process, just a change in perception.

Let's start here.

Think about your hair. Think about your fingernails. Think about the blood that flows throughout your body. All of these bodily existences have something in common.

Think about it.

Whenever you lose any of these items which live within the world of everything, these items have the ability to replenish themselves. Think about it. As far as the replenishment, where does it come from? Where does the new hair come from? Where do the new nails come from? How does the blood replenish itself? Where does it come from? Let's ask some deeper questions.

Take a tree and its leaves. Where did it come from?

Think about the ground around the tree. Look how big and tall an oak tree gets. As an oak tree grows, you would think that the oak tree would take its resources for its content from the surrounding ground. But yet as big as an oak tree is, where did it get its content or substance. Where did the structure of the tree come from? The mass? Is it magic? Did the tree use the soil as the base of its substance? If it did, as the tree grows, the surrounding ground and soil would begin to be displaced and would disappear and reform into the tree. This is not the case though. So, where did the mass of the tree come from?

Where does the new hair, nail, and blood cells come from in your body? From where do they regenerate? From what ground source does it derive its content and substance? What base? Just like the tree, since the ground is still full, from what does the stump of the tree get its form and content? What makes the bark? What makes the branches, the leaves, and in some cases even the fruit of the tree?

After a few years from planting, there might be enough fruit in a tree to feed hundreds of people, but there stands a massive tree where before, nothing existed. The only thing that went into that space over the years is water.

Could it be? Did everything that is now seen in terms of all the components of the tree emanate from water? Think about it. Even the makeup of your body is almost 85% to 95% water. The new segments of your body, your hair, your fingernails, your blood, as it replenishes itself, is based on some type of continual instruction or information pushing water into multiple formations.

All living substances are sustained by water! All living substances emanate from water!

Let's go just a little further.

Let's say that you plant four different trees next to each other. You plant an apple tree, a lemon tree, a cherry tree and a pecan tree. Each tree has its own seed, which is very tiny, but will soon be massive trees with hundreds of fruits produced. Every seed in the ground receives the same water to start, but over time, as each tree grows, the trees take on different shapes and produces very different fruit, but all emanate from the same base - water. Wow!

How does the molecules and cells divide into the various shapes and colors, with different fruit flavors and textures, all providing a variance of different experiences? What directs the water into such different formations? Where does the instructions come from? Where does the information come from?

Let's look closer at these two words. Instruct and Inform. A structure does not become a structure without in-struction. A form does not become form without in-form-ation. All of this is contained within the seed. The power of the instructions and the information within the seed to direct the "water" molecule is incredible to say the least. All living and growing structures develop from this same model.

Here, water is fluid in nature, and based on the instructions and information that come from the seed, the water moves into place, then the molecules and cells are constructed and reformed into the various formations to be what it is called to be along with its base minerals and carbon.

Just as water is fluid in nature awaiting instructions and information to become a tree or a plant; energy, the invisible base for all life, also waits for instruction and information. Here, as far as energy is concerned, energy is not formed into a structure based on what's in a seed, but what's in your mind. Your mind works on the same bases as a seed directing water. Your mind directs energy.

All biological systems stem from the movement of water and then the placement of water, and in the same way, all physical systems, both animate and inanimate stem from the movement and placement of invisible energy systems, but the instructions and information have its birth place in your mind. Yes, I am saying it. Your thoughts are like seeds.

So, perception is our gift to order the very energy of life. Many people do not realize that their perception formulates a brood of thoughts, and this brood of thoughts formulate a brood of energy systems, and these energy systems construct and formulate a brood of things which then become the basis of your experience. Your purpose in life stems from what you think. Here, you have full control!

Perception is our gift to order the very energy of life.

Again, just as a seed directs water, thoughts direct energy into structure and form. All energy systems that are directed from you via your thoughts are now in a relationship with what comes from you.

Let's look at the seed again. Within the seed is the total picture of the tree which is to be formed out of that seed. In essence, the full form of the tree exists in the seed waiting for the water to fill out the form. In the same way, your thoughts immediately become who you are. The energy added to you, are the thoughts become the structure and form of what already is in non-matter.

This is why perception is most powerful. Everyone has equal access to energy, but everyone's perception is different.

As I said earlier, becoming who you are starts with discovering who you are, and since everything outside of your mind is made of the same basic substance, and you control the energy which controls the water that make up the physical existences, you then control that which becomes the basis of your experience. All of this in turn gives you definition and purpose. This discovery starts with uncovering the capabilities of your mind. And you are what you perceive yourself to be. This is who and what you are.

Becoming who you are starts with discovering who you are.

Everything is everything. And everything is you. Your only job is to control the arrangement of you.

Dealing with What's Wrong

What interferes with your perception? What stops you from progressing in life? Why do things go backwards sometimes despite your best efforts? I call it torment. Or things that torment. Torment derives from the same energy in which you have full control and arrangement over.

Torment is continual unsatisfactory experiences in which, when you experience them, you don't quite know how to handle. They can be any type of hardships, annoyances, or things and events that become laborious. You can also consider them as your failures and disappointments.

Now you must understand that under the guise of taking full responsibility, you have to recognize that these negative events derive also out of your very own perception. It's all about how you relate to these events. You can give rise to the purpose and the meaning of these events. You can make these events who you are, or you can face them with a level of determination and redefine them immediately by your thoughts and then follow up with immediate actions.

I call it "Squaring Up" to what you are facing and to what you are feeling at times. You have to make what you are facing and feeling speechless (vibration wise), thusly stripping it of its definition by using the power of your perception. In other words, you have the power to silence the noise of what's wrong in front of you by redirecting your attention.

First, you must understand that there are two distinct presences before you at all times. They are the presence of what you want and the presence of what you do not want. To start, I want to clue you into the fact that the presence of what you want is more readily available to you than the presence of what you do not want. If this is true, how does one experience a great deal of what they don't want in life?

Remember, I equated the human mind with a seed and the mind is created to produce what's in it, just like a seed. If you look at Earth's history and what it has produced over eons of time, seeds have been accurate in producing after its kind in every segment of nature. So, the human mind, being an advanced seed form, has within it the experience of exacting production after its kind based on what's in it.

Believe me, the science of this has been developed over billions of years and is scientifically exacting, accurate, and precise in its production. Nothing that is ever produced comes about without a mind to make it happen. That's why life is never random. This ultimately may seem to be complicated, but I will strip away the complexity of this, because the big question is, why do things happen to you that seem to not have been planned by you? And then, what control do you have over these situations?

First of all, you have to take responsibility towards the presence of what you want in life and not focus on the presence of what you don't want. All life is meant to produce after its kind. Biologically, if you wanted a baby and you were pregnant, nine months after conception you would not as a human produce a baby cow or a chicken. That's because all physical systems take responsibility in producing after its kind. The mind does the same thing.

Let's look at this word – conception, as it relates to perception. Conception proceeds perception. The prefix of this word is per-, which means complete. Ception- which is the root of both words means "to gather". Conceive is to take into the mind. Perceive is to complete what's in the mind. All of this is a work that takes place in the mind before anything is produced.

To be in line with billions of years of evolution, as humans, it is a correct biological and scientific operation to want something and then produce it. Meaning, you are supposed to desire a new car and produce it, a beautiful home and produce it, financial advancement and produce it, diamonds and produce it, gold and produce it, a super business venture and produce it, travel and produce it, etc. Get the point. But we can conceive it, but a lot of times we don't perceive it for production.

As humans, and within the human mind, we are the only entity that can produce after its kind, but then can change our minds based on what we face in front of us and then produce something else. A lemon seed can't stop being a lemon tree, a hawk can't stop being a hawk, but a human can change its mind and move into an entirely different direction.

We can conceive a dream, but at the moment of adversity, based on what is allowed to take place within the mind, things can shift, and we experience what we don't like or want. Torment.

Now, keep in mind what I said earlier, you have a responsibility towards the presence of what you want in life. But when you relate to the torment that might be presented to you, your responsibility actually shifts to what you think is wrong in life. Here, at that very moment, what is conceived is not perceived. What exist in its completeness, because you are now adding into the "mind mix" other values and absences that have nothing to do with what you want, it now presents itself as incomplete. These other values I call torment. So, what is produced is incomplete or presented back to you as torment or tormenting.

Torment is having one thing in your mind and living something else outside of your mind. The reason why torment is so tormenting, is that deep within you, you know that everything you need to accomplish what you want in life actually exist, but you are distant from its presence by being distracted by what you don't want. Most people handle this by just becoming comfortable with what is not quite right, and then become a professional at living at this undesirable level and state.

But I'll say it again, you have a responsibility to the good you want in your life. You have a responsibility to be successful. The Earth has successfully completed its journey of successful production over 13.5 billion years, now the whole of creation is waiting for you to know your ability to create success, and then after that, more success.

Where does the presence of what you don't want come from, and more importantly, how do you face it or "Square Up" to it? This is where perception comes into play.

Staying Complete

Perception is about keeping your conception complete until it is produced into reality. In order to be, you have to be faced with the possibility of "not to be", and "not to be" has its own production system when that becomes your focus. In order to fully experience complete success, the possibility for failure has to exist. Both what is and what is not, makes its appearance at the same time. Sometimes "what is not" or what you do not have in mind to happen to you might seem to present itself beyond your control, and you can assign to this notion these factors: what others might say or do, catastrophic events of nature, sudden change in the financial climate, loss of status in a close relationship, sudden illnesses, and the like.

Holding on to a complete picture in your head of what you want will cause you to see beyond these undesired eventful presentations no matter how poignant and prominent these eventful presentations might seem at the time of its inception. You have to "square up" to these inceptions with your conception staying intact by maintaining full control of your perception. No outer tangible event can rule what exist in non-matter, which is what's in your mind. What's in your mind can't be touched.

Again, "not to be" or what you don't want in life has its own production system. Both what you dream of and the potential for failure are planted in the mind, one can't exist without the other. But the mind is so perfect, it can produce either one. This is because the mind is a seed, and the energy is like the water. Your mind is in a constant state of production. The key here is directing the energy.

If you direct your energy towards the problem, your solution will die with it. You cannot create a solution for a problem, because solutions for all problems already exist in nature. Any attempt to solve a problem brings you into relationship with that very problem, and your problem will grow versus your dream growing. Staying focused and acting on the completed picture of your dream will eliminate nagging issues by default. You can only know the truth of this when what you want in life becomes more real in you than any perceived reality outside of you.

Perception is about holding onto a complete picture. Insight is always there and can become a fun vehicle of transformation as you watch "wrong" things present themselves to you for your consideration. No matter what is presented to you, you can maintain full control of the arrangement of your thoughts in your mind. Clear insight forces foresight, which is the ability to see beyond any type of negative event or presentation.

The true beauty of this is that you can then watch physically how all the Earth systems are designed to obey the energy emitting from you based on your perception. A seed will always produce after its kind, and a tree will always produce fruit after its kind, thusly your mind will always produce after its kind. The key here is this, instead of getting involved with the problem, look for the relationship that will fertilize the seed of your insight and stop relating to the problem.

Clear insight forces foresight.

There is much more goodness presented to you at all times than bad, but it is your perception that creates the energy which will bring one or the other into focus. Your responsibility is to your dream, because what you don't want in life is just a diversion and not a reality. A problem only becomes a problem and a reality when you agree with it by relating to it. You have to stop letting outside events destroy the complete pictures of your inner vision. There is always something good to relate to that matches your in-vision and your insight, and it is that relationship that moves you to the degree mark that leads to your success. Say to yourself and to anyone present, "I'm not here to solve a problem, I am here to build a relationship".

But most importantly, you must master creating complete visions in the mind and gain the ability to hold that vision. Holding the vision helps bring into focus your provision.

"I'm not here to solve a problem, I am here to build a relationship".

Provision

Provision is the answer to your perception. It is taking account of the physical things that match your mental things. I call it imaging. Every successful corporation does it, and you can do it in your personal life to gain anything you desire in life. Provision is a powerful concept that many people fail to use in trying to obtain their goals. Provision is the proactive action towards what's in you by accounting those things that match your vision outside of you.

The key here is keying into the knowledge that there is always some "thing" available that matches your inner vision. You have to practice seeing. Involvement with any "thing" that doesn't match your inner vision will block you from seeing what is really there that promotes your true destiny. This is why it is vital that as you become clear about your vision, you must document it.

Being clear is vital to the concept of provision. Things are provided that match your vision, but if you are unclear about your vision, it is hard to gain sight of those very things. How do you become clear? How do you reach a state of clear?

Purposeful Environment

First you must set yourself at an advantage to gain clear knowledge. Your environment plays an important role in gaining clarity of mind and perspective. "Quite" is the quick road to clear. But here, I am not talking strictly in terms of sound. There are a lot of noise to be experienced without a single sound being made. Your brain is always at work processing information. Some items are harder to process than others. It's like a computer, when you try to retrieve vital information that you desire from your computer, if there are a lot of other processes taking place simultaneously, the information or the file you are trying to retrieve comes up much slower than it needs to.

Now using the same computer analogy, there are times when other programs in the computer that are running background processes, even if the programs themselves are not activated. I call these programs dead programs, because they are dead weight, yet they are active. All of this is taking up computer memory. The more of this that is taking place as background "noise", the more the computer's vital resources are being taken up. Much of this activity has nothing to do generally with whatever task is at hand. Again, I call this – background noise. The mind works in much the same way. Many times, there are a lot of background noises and processes that have nothing to do with a task at hand. So, the effort to pull up desired information is slowed up considerably.

The best way to do this is to create a purposeful environment. What is a purposeful environment? A purposeful environment is basically an environment where all "things" or items serve a specific clear purpose. In this environment there are no items around that you generally can't give definition to. It's not having a room full of stuff that has nothing to do with nothing, and it's not having a contingency of persons around you that are aimless and directionless.

You should be able to look at any of the first ten items around you that you see, and each one should have immediate meaning and purpose. Every item has to have current usefulness. Nothing should be outdated and stagnant. Every paper, every book, every electronic device, every piece of furniture, every tool, every picture, every fixture etc., must be current, purposeful, and useful.

Why?

Whether you realize it or not, every "thing" around you speaks. When an item comes into your line of site, it tells you what it is, and it speaks to you its purpose. Your mind is so intricate that it is in a constant state of coming into agreement with something at all times. This creates a dialogue or a noise/sound system.

When you ask yourself, "what is my purpose in life?" you would need to get a clear precise answer so that answer can be correctly acted upon. But when your continuous dialogue around you is consistently unclear, it then becomes hard to push past all of the noise to get to clear answers about your own self.

Another way to put this is that your mind is in a continuous state of answering. For example, your mind sees a light fixture and your mind says that this is a light fixture. That light fixture has to say yes "I AM" in order to be what your mind says it is to be. Your mind then answers yes in agreement in anticipation of a relationship based on the expectation of that device's performance. Whether now or later, when you need to act upon that agreement, and you approach that same light fixture, you then begin whatever process to activate the light. When the fixture doesn't produce any light, this immediately creates a dialogue of crisis adjustment in your mind that becomes "louder" than its intended purpose, because you are now dealing with a disagreement and then trying to adjust, versus building and adding to your purpose.

Notice here though, your mind is doing all of the defining, answering and agreements. If you have thirty items surrounding you and only five of them actually served a purpose, have an immediate meaning, and is useful in some way, your mind still recognizes all thirty items, then your proportion of useful thinking is only five parts good to twenty five parts of dead weight. A lot of brain space is being tasked with erroneous "noise", causing the good sound to be diminished. There is a great deal of erroneous exchange even though the process seems negligible or operating in the background. Clear your spaces!

If you then ask yourself, "what is my purpose in life?", you couldn't even begin to answer that clearly because your continual dialogue is crowded with purposeless sound. Even if you did come up with an answer, it will most likely match the negative dead dialogue around you.

Imagine this when it comes to people. Imagine purposeless, non-useful, and meaningless people around you as a majority. The funny thing is, is that they can actually speak and act into you their nothingness and non-clarity. This is dangerous to your personal clarity. Becoming clear about your life starts with clearing your spaces.

How many television shows do you watch that are aimless? How many places do you go that are non-productive? There are even some religious activities that have no real bottom line that can produce anything useful. What music do you listen to that actually has meaning? Who do you speak to on a daily basis, that when the conversation is over you are actually on another level or your life takes on a deeper meaning? Clear? All of this dialogue, just like a computer, is stored as memory.

Clearance

Clearance. This must take place. The process of clearing. Removing all the "no's" from your environment. Once you have done this job, you can now ask questions about your personal goals and direction, and then define them. Here you can validate your mind with good memory which assists you in becoming clear. When the "things" create definite responsive "yes's" around you, the memory of these "yes's" assist in the knowledge of all the "yes's" that already reside within you.

You are complete inside. Everyone is. The point is, is that not everyone experiences their own completeness. The only way to experience the completeness inside you is the proper arrangement of matching items outside you to be experienced. This is what imaging is all about. Imaging is about what mirrors the true complete picture inside you.

Even when you don't like something, the not liking of the some "thing" is proof that there is something in you that you do like. You just have to learn the reference points in order to see it. You could not feel incomplete without there being completeness to reference it against. Feeling bad about something, or bad about some results, or bad about somebody is still good news, because this "bad" is referenced off of a complete state that is calling out to you to be better, which is the birth place of desire. When bad presents itself, do not focus on the matching feeling inside you. Realize that the resonation of the bad has to resonate off of something that is good because all "bad" has to have a reference point in order to be defined as bad. Quickly identify this good, even if it is not physically present, make that your focus, and then make sure that all subsequent relationships match the "good".

Desire resonates off of your completeness, whether you see or understand your completeness or not. You have to become clear about what is in you, and then the power resides in your ability to then arrange those things outside of yourself to match you. Again, it is a responsibility and a duty to match yourself. This is the process of imaging. Matching the good in you creates a better world for others.

Matching the good in you creates a better world for others.

Everything since the dawn of the Universe images after its kind. We as humans are the only entity that can image from non-existence. That's why truly creative and successful people defy current existences to create something new. Existing circumstances, situations, and issues cannot compete with what is in them.

You have to engrain this knowledge, what's outside of you cannot compete with what's in you. Your core existence is good, and you exist to produce more good. Anything bad that you perceive did not come from you, but was introduced to you as possibility. And without being clear, you could entertain what's not versus what is.

What's outside of you cannot compete with what's inside you.

Clear your environment.
See the good. This is your Ah ha moment.
The next task is the match up the good outside of you.

Lines of Intelligence

Now you must begin the matching game or the process of imaging what's outside you. At this point you may begin to see that things are actually in existence to match your inside. You must take account of these things so that they don't slip by you or away from you.

The most important factor when it comes to imaging is what I call Lines of Intelligence. This line starts with a clear vision of what you want to take place in your life. Let's think about a few types of lines to make this concept clear. You can have an electrical line or a plumbing line. In each case, each line acts as a conduit which carries its substance from one point to its desired point of destination. Also, in both cases the line is not a singular line. The lines primarily consist of several types and levels of conduits connected together to achieve one goal, and that is to get the substance that it contains to its desired point of destination for its intended use and purpose. In both cases all conduits must be open at every point for the electricity or water to flow through.

At any point, when any individual conduit is closed or blocked, the flow stops at that point. Under these conditions the intended purpose of the substance is never realized. People are conduits for your purpose and I always state, "Don't let your dreams die at the next person". You have to surround yourself with the right people in order to create Lines of Intelligence. Your dreams, your desire, your vision and goals are intelligent facts and they must have a clear line of conduits to reach its destination and intended purpose. Not everybody can carry your dream or accept its content for whatever reason. Communication with these types of people must be kept at a minimum or none at all.

Don't let your dreams die at the next person.

Another example of a Line of Intelligence is a 4x4 relay track team. Each person must have the same destination in mind along with the intent of optimum performance in order for the unit to realize its goal. Anyone that is not on the same page can cost the team the race. Anybody that you relay the information to that comes from within you, should carry that information from you with the utmost responsiveness and respect for what's coming from you, along with the plans and intentions of playing a full, competent role of helping you reach your destination and fulfill your purpose.

Many of your dreams and destinies die at the next person, because your intensive intelligence is passed on to people who can't see you, whether those persons intend not to see you, or they are just ignorant of the possibilities coming from you. Having good people around you who are both comprehensive and responsive creates a strong Line of Intelligence.

Having all of this in place creates a morphic field for your dreams to thrive from inception, to conception, and then reception; anything else is deception. And I mean anything else!

With your environment and people now set, it is time to gather in what you have correctly perceived as being your next station in life. Everything is documented and you have set Lines of Intelligence. You now must begin to put the external pieces together that represent your internal picture. First, you begin by not believing, but knowing that it all exists. With a more communicative environment and agreeable personages around you, these things can be more readily identified.

Expectations & Marking Expectations

Here, you develop expectation. Expectation begins with identification. Along with a clear vision, you must be clear on what it takes to complete your journey. When this is done, every day will provide you with matching material to your inner being. The day has to do it.

Why is there such a thing as a day? What is the purpose of days? A day consists of one complete rotation of the Earth. The sun, moon and the stars help us mark the day. Why? Day is about measurement and not a function of time. In order to really understand this, associate the day with light. And I mean literal light. At every full turn of the Earth, light makes its way back around to you in its fullness. We do know this, that the Day delivers light. The only thing that is faster than the speed of light is the speed of thought. Thought is the only entity that can precede light.

There are two possible thoughts here. Light is random or light is organized. Since light can be measured, it must be organized. Organized by thought. Each day proves that. Light emanating from the sun is definite and can be taken in by structured devices and organized into useful energy. Something answers every thought and we see proof of it every day. Every thought is provided for each and every day.

The day is the basic rudiment of measurement and the structure of time is about marking points or appoints that are set for your success. What marks or measures your day, or what marks light? The sun, moon and stars are the initial existences that determine set measurements or marks. This is what the day initially brings. But marks are always representative of something called out to be. Existence has to be marked in order for it to be experienced. Your thoughts are markers. Your thoughts are re-mark-able.

Existence has to be marked in order for it to be experienced.

Let's go here. Even the basic MRI machines prove that at every thought, energy is emitted. This is determined by the light images that are produced as it maps points of the brain when a patient think certain types of thought. This "thought-energy" is a mark, although subtle, this energy has the same level of produced representation as a star, the moon, or even the sun that marks the Day. After the thought emanates from you, the resulting energy pattern is set into the Universe forever and takes its place into the cycles of creation and production. The value of this mark is equally valuable as every other substance that exists.

As the Day cycles, it is set to pick up the measurements of everything in existence. The Day is representative of all cycles in existence and serves as the base for all other cycles in existence that extends from solar and lunar cycles to frequencies represented in sound and light, as everything cycles into a production. The Day, like the MRI machine picks up on your every thought, and much like the MRI machine, the Day begins the process of producing the image of your very thoughts.

Your very energy system sets the tone that activates many cycles on many levels that line up to your energy platform. Every Day is set to present the resulting spins back to the originator via many different levels of presentation, because every resulting energy pattern is a mirror of the originator, which is you.

Now I am speaking factually not esoterically, because most of our technology today is based on the same factual principles, which is precise and accurate in its presentation as it mirrors the originating source. Every satellite signal, radio signal, FM signal, gamma ray, infrared, 4g, 5g, LTE, and bluetooth, all work on this exact principle. The Day, being the chief cycle, is prepared to present to you a physical representation of your thought in every way and this is guaranteed. So, live with extreme positive expectation.

I tell people, "Watch how you start your day". The Day will always present to you pieces of mirrored-existence based on your thoughts. You must start your day with you and expectations of timed presentations that mirror you and your desired destiny. If you start your day without expectation, you will miss all these marked points of presentation. This is the basis of provision. Just as the sun marks itself through consistent presentation, as it is also with the stars, the moon, zodiac patterns and many more basic cycles; the things based off your thoughts, cycle from your initial energy patterns forever into the Universe.

You must be open to what each day brings based on expectancy. When you look at your TV guide and a show is listed to come on at a specific time period and on a specific channel, you pick up the remote control and tune into the channel with full expectancy of the presentation that was stated in the guide. As you scroll down the TV guide containing hundreds of listed channels, each channel, as you tune in has accurate presentations of what is listed. These channels cycle in on frequencies, whether by satellite or by fiber optic cables. Your thoughts are deposited forever in the subtle energy systems and travels through a more brute energy system that are all ready for rebroadcasting back to you, but only as you tune in to the correct corresponding station. Your Desire!

Nothing that you think is ever lost. Have you ever thought of a great idea in passing, but because you weren't tuned into you, several years later you see someone on TV presenting that same idea and you said "Hey! That's my idea!"? Yes, someone has possibly picked up on your very energy channel that you set. And much like cable companies that are shooting out to you signals or marked existences in High Definition, you must learn to pick up your own return signals in High Definition.

Yes, your every thought is literally provided for because it really becomes its own provision. Once you lock into these provisions and can see them in High Definition, it is time to produce.

Production

Production is a matter of intimacy. Production is a matter of passion. The key here is that you have a responsibility to produce. The quintessence character of the Universe is results, and at the core of the Universe, at the basis of its existence is production. Production is at the foundation of all experience.

The nature of the Universe is to act with precision and the Universe is very accurate in its presentations and representations. The only turn in this level of precision is in the human mind. What can get in the way of precision is decision or the ability to decide, specifically the ability to decide more or act towards more. "More" is essential to all life. Nothing rarely stays the same except for what governs the ability for the Universe to continue to expand and grow.

Your very nature is to expand and grow. Included in this process is decision making. Decision-making coupled with agreement, meaning, and what comes from another's mind or action from another corresponding to your decisions is the seat of all power. This is the process that leads to production, which is fundamental to expansion and growth. You are meant to produce. You are built for production.

Your very nature is to expand and grow.

Every Day brings the supply for production. It is your responsibility to be all you can be, primarily for other human minds to grow. What do I mean by this?

Imaging

We are now back to the concept of imaging. Every existence on Earth produces after its kind, but in order for the human mind to produce, it needs basic images in order to do so. Where do these images come from? They come from previous minds and accomplishments. The greater you live, the greater those who come after you can live. But this comes to be even more important if you have children or other close personages that are influential.

This is also important if you are in any type of leadership position whether that leadership is practiced within a corporation, religion, political settings etc. Your image of optimal production is imaged onto others and serves as a base to their creativity, which moves all of existence to higher levels. What you produce plays a vital role to all life and not just your own.

What you produce plays a vital role to all life and not just your own.

That's why the rule of the Universe is set for your success and not failure. Again, the only thing that brings about failure is a component within the human mind. We are the only entity that can decide into non-production. The laws of the Universe are imminent and immutable, which means that they cannot be changed. Energy is a constant and can only be directed. The neat thing here is that you are privileged with the ability to direct and order energy. How well you do this is predicated on your decision-making ability and what agreements you draw into the process.

Passion

Here, passion is central to the whole process. But passion as you might understand it is not applicable here. The passion I am speaking of is created passion. Most times when you set plans or a goal, your body and what's inside you are not prepared to go along. Why? What is set in your mind has to also be set into many other dimensions also. This requires work. Work sets energy. You just can't make a decision to accomplish an end goal, you must also align all existing entities and energies around you to accomplish the reaching of your destination.

Many people look at passion as an inner drive. But before you can drive, you must build the car. Passion is not a feeling. Passion is a system of habits designed and accepted by you that become the basis of bringing something new into existence. A lot of things that you would need to do to bring about a good result, generally speaking, you are not going to feel like doing it. This is why so many people are distant from their accomplishments, because they are waiting for a feeling to come to get them going.

Feelings are built just like anything else. You must build your passion on purpose versus waiting for it to come to you. You must create passion to set new patterns for production. You must do this until the things that you need to do in order to reach your goals become automatic. It is this automaticy that is your passion. Passion is what you do without thinking, hence, the true definition of passion – what's done without thinking. The more you do something, the more it becomes a part of you and what you are, thusly removing thought, and now then is your passion - good or bad, healthy or unhealthy, wanted or unwanted.

The key component to passion is intimacy. Why do I use the word intimacy when it comes to passion and production? Intimacy denotes close relations to something with the focus of production. True passion becomes extended into greatness when it is shared in order to produce a result.

It takes two to make a baby, even if it's a test-tube baby; the doctor has to still be in agreement with the mother in order for something to happen or be produced. Where do your agreements take you? Who are you intimate with when it comes to your destiny? A High Definition life means that you are clear about all these things. The people you relate to become your story.

The people you relate to become your story.

You can trace all of your end results back to the relationships you choose. The success of any major corporation or project always hinge on how well people work together and how often they make good connections that lead to results and production. Ok. Let's get into it.

Engage in What's For You

There is an inherent beauty in differences and diversification. We all are unique as individuals. Things are divided to gain identification; they are joined to gain qualification. Quality extends from like-mindedness. The quality of your life is not based solely on how good you are, but the quality of your production. The quality of all production stems from the level and quality of integration with other persons. Again, people here have to view your goals with respect, and respect starts with positive acknowledgement and intimate action towards your destiny.

Not only must you be passionate about where you are going, but the people around you in which you choose to relate to must carry that same passion. Here a "feeling towards" is not sufficient, but it takes habitual action that engrains a pattern of active attention towards the processes of your goal. This type of passion or attention bypasses all distractive options that lead to minimal accomplishments.

Here, you must create the first image of passion that people can pick upon. Oooohhh K?

Intelligence and ignorance exist simultaneously at the same time and they are the basis for all energy directives, ordering, and flow. Answers to any end-point always exist. You either create patterns of picking up on intelligence or what I call accurate information, or you pick up on inaccurate information. There is no in between.

When you become clear on your next quest for production, sig-nals for that end result are set into subtle energy systems that produce what you are looking for right away. But when you look out into the physical world for your result, you do not immediately see your result. What you actually see is a diversification of supply and people. You see a multiplicity of things. Passion is when you set the pictures so well inside yourself that the multiplicities of what you see in diversification begin to choose to be like you and become a singularity that mirrors you.

This is why it is important to stick to your guns about what it takes to get where you are going, even when the ones you love don't match up. Passion will move you past this unmatched existence. Intima-cy here is the key. There is a reason why humans don't have sex with bears, cows, chickens, porky pines, squirrels and the like in order to have a baby.

Intimacy becomes a factor here, because when you consider inti-macy, you take into account who and what you are intimate with. Intimacy denotes the intent to produce, and intimacy can't occur with just anybody or anything. Again, we are not designed to mate with anything and everything, and much in the same way it is dangerous to be intimate with anyone who does not have the same mind as yourself.

Moreover, eating a dirt patty can't do for you what a nice salad can do. A glass of gasoline can't be as refreshing and beneficial as a good glass of fresh orange juice. You can't converse with everything that is diverse. There is purpose and order to everything in existence. Life answers our every call, but a great deal of the time, we choose into what is not intellectually optimal for our destiny by selecting an existence of ignorance to relate to and then engage in what is not for us, and then expect to produce results. It won't happen.

When someone is in disagreement with you, you must recognize that at that point, you might as well be talking to another species of animal. In our humanity, the structure of our biological make-up is 99.99% the same from person to person, but a simple mind difference reconstructs a difference in likeness to staggering proportions. What's worse, is that a person can tell you what you want to hear and say that they support you, but can be so inherently different than your purpose, that using the analogy of the difference between apples and oranges would only scratch the surface. When we choose to relate to something so different and with people who are not in agreement, production becomes entirely impossible.

But in the same light, what makes the human mind so intriguing is that within the very diversity of human existence, you can find likeness using the same mind. This is why imaging is vital. Imaging provides a picture of end results. When people can get a good picture of your destiny, they can within their differences reach a common goal.

If you want to build a house, a team made totally of accountants wouldn't be able to get the job done. A team made totally of contractors wouldn't be able to get the job done. A team made totally of suppliers wouldn't be able to get the job done. A team made totally of electricians wouldn't be able to get the job done. But a team that comprises of these individual and diverse talents together can get the job done.

When a multiplicity of talented, diverse, people pick up on the same image and agree, then multiplication can take place that leads to a higher quality of life. But you must set the pattern or the image, and this takes passion. Passion has to be a switch from ignorance to intelligence. Intelligence is deciding what works for you, recognizing within the day what works for you, and then foremost, engaging what works for you.

Passion About What Works

Generally, our passion develops over time based on past histori-cal events that contribute to what I call our "inner movie". That movie becomes what we know; thusly it is what we then become passionate about. Have you ever wondered why an abused woman would insist on staying with her abuser? Well over time, maybe seeing her father abuse women, and then living through abuse herself, this becomes her "inner movie", she can then appear passionate about staying with what is not working.

In business and personal development, people do it all the time. They stick with what doesn't work. Their "inner movie" and the result-ing self-images will cause them not to see or recognize during the course of the day what is good for them although the good is readily available. In this case, a different passion has to be developed when you see yourself not getting the results you want.

Again, you must really understand that passion here is not a feel-ing. Feeling is just one result that stem from passion. Even at this point; motivational techniques, meditations, religious sacraments, prayer, and the like cannot instill different end results. The process to create new passion is quite simple from the standpoint of process but can be difficult from the stand point of decision making.

First, you must identify someone who has reached a similar goal you are attempting to reach. Get their story if they are willing to share. The best place to do this with exacting accuracy is a bookstore. But reading the book will not instill a new passion, practicing the book will. Write down points of practice and do them throughout your day. This is intelligence. As a matter of fact, this is the beginning of establishing your line of intelligence because you are pulling from the success images of others who came before you. This is about active practicing. Only the practice of the things they have done establishes a memory-base to spurn new channels of passion.

As time passes, doing what successful people do will become au-tomatic. The height of this notion is demonstrated when outside images and events that are not in agreement with your direction are ignored because of the level of "automicy" that is built within you to be on another level. Nothing stands in your way. Your behavior patterns are set in stone. Someone can even suggest to you to take specific actions that are not related to your destiny and you readily turn them down.

When this type energy is set, it becomes incredibly easier to recognize people, events, places and the like that have been readied to advance your inner causes. It is with these that you become intimate with. Like I said, the Day presents these auto-structures that line up with your intellect, because it is the Days duty to provide them at the inception of your desire. When you change your position from ignorance to intelligence and set your passion, and you have built the right relationships, this will create a greater energy vortex that will assist the Day in arranging like energy.

Here's a small example. Have you ever had a deep desire to punch somebody in the face? It is just that day when somebody out of nowhere decides to get on your nerves. This type of energy alignment happens at every point of setting intentions or desire, both good and bad.

Relationship Investments

Investments in your relationships are the biggest investments you can make. It is the first level of your personal arrangements that is economic in nature. Just as imaging is vital, the principle of "Returning" becomes paramount to your personal development and production. When you look in the mirror, because of its reflective properties and correct lighting, the mirror will return to you an image of yourself, and with this image, you can tell who you are in more detail. This is what people bring to you when it comes to the principle of returning and imaging. What do people return to you based on what you put out?

Here, I would like to investigate the word – honor. This is a good place to practice developing your passion. Choosing relationships should be based on choosing those who return to you or honor you. What is it that the person is returning? Your image. You should look for "you" in people's action towards you. Anything outside of this, you are being robbed. This is why ignorance in this case can be deadly to your destiny.

Choosing relationships should be based on choosing those who return to you and honor you.

People honor you by knowing what your needs are and are actively making an effort to be a supply to you. Along with this, you must also practice honoring others. This type of co-returning sets the stage for your vision to be opened up to your life supply on a daily basis.

Progression

Everything in your life must progress. Just like production, progression is a duty and responsibility, not only for your own benefit, but also for the benefit of others. Progression is an automatic result once you master the first three principles of High Definition Life – perception, provision, and production. Mastery of these will allow them to work as a well-oiled machine.

Progression is closely associated with growth. Your personal growth in all your endeavors has to be closely monitored. Your growth tells a story. Your growth is your story. When it comes to growing and what can block your growth in any area, we face some of the same issues that we find with production.

Here, you must even the more, monitor the activities around you, especially the activities of others around you. Growth is an energy process and anything or persons with unlike energy will block your own growth. It is hard to appreciate the value of this because of the value we give to energy systems around us that aren't optimally beneficial to our personal existence.

How does this so easily become the case?

Growth is an energy process and anything or any persons with unlike energy will stunt your own growth.

The Value of Energy - Volume Versus Content

There are two ways you can value energy – by volume and by content. A lot of times we mistake the volume of energy for the content of energy. This is dangerous. This is why you have to have a clear purpose defined for your end goals, because the present energies or your surrounding energy systems have to carry the content of your purpose.

Non-conducive environments can easily stagnate your growth. This stagnation can easily be missed because of your involvement with the volume of energy, even if that energy has no content that adds value to your direction. In other words, you can have a whole lot going on, while simultaneously going nowhere – "The Treadmill Effect". This is because we make the mistake of engaging energy sources that seem to incite activity, but with no active production, and without production there cannot be any growth.

I call energy sources light sources. You have to ask the question when it comes to any type of engagement, whether it be people, places or things; does this bring light to my efforts? What also must be recognized here is that energy can also foster dark properties, but still have the same sensory effects as light-based energy. Why is this?

Any energy that has the same volume, light or dark can have the exact same effect, but it is the content of the energy that affects. This is why you have to pay attention and measure the results of your engagements and not necessarily the engagement itself. You have to monitor your growth. The worst feeling to have in life is when you put a lot of energy into something or somebody and nothing happens. There is no return. Content has to be the staple of how you value things.

Content has to be the staple of how you value things and people.

Looking for evidence should become a foundational principle, because the presentation of anything or anyone is not necessarily the presentation of content.

Many people have been robbed and ripped off in many different ways because of this same illusion. They mistake volume for content. When a woman sees an attractive guy, all chiseled out, finely dressed, and with a flurry of intoxicating words, falls into a level of engagement, and forgets to measure the content of the man verses the volume of the man, she is then easily taken. How many people watching a television commercial, then buys a product off of TV that looks so robust and effective, but when they open the box and plug it up or try it on, the performance is weak?

How many people looking for business opportunities get involved with some of the weakest business ventures just because the presentation was sensational? Evidence has to play a role in everything you do. Substance is key and volume doesn't determine content.

Evidence has to play a role in everything you do.

Evidence of Growth

Let's get back to growth. Evidence is about the growth of a thing and not a presentation of the thing. Why is it important to monitor growth in others and the growth in things? Growth denotes good energy, even if there is little volume. It's the difference in looking at a picture of a plant and looking at an actual live plant. Because of the volume of what you see, you can get a general initial response of joy based on what is seen. But because one is live and the other is just a picture, you can only glean a greater experience from the live plant because you can witness the evidence of its content as it grows.

Evidence is about growth and not presentation. The live plant carries with it, active energy, which is good energy. The other is just a picture. Some people can paint a good picture to get you excited but can't do anything for you. Stop getting involved with images that have no content. These images carry no intrinsic value to your wealth and health.

When you look at a live plant versus a mere picture of a plant, you are actually looking at the total journey of that plant. The live plant had to grow to get to that point. Not only is this important, the journey of the plant to that point also denotes that it is capable of continued growth. This is something in which you can put your faith in because of the evidence. The energy of the content, which causes the growth, is energy that can be mirrored inside you that will teach and enhance your inner being along with your own aspirations towards growth.

When you engage empty people, you will be left with the feeling of emptiness. If you were starving and you were dying to eat some food, let's say breakfast, and somebody proclaimed, "I will get you breakfast", and then they returned with a picture of breakfast, complete with all the fixins', what good does a picture of a breakfast do you?

Growth is a staple of the Universe, so why would you in any way position yourself not to grow? Everything and every person around you must be growing in some way. This has to be the law of your life. If not, dark energy will remain present. But yet dark energy is still an active energy and it will draw on your energy to maintain itself. The difference is, is that nothing is being returned to you.

The principle of return is a principle that needs to be activated in your life. The fundiment of the Universe is not just give and take; but give, take, and growth. The expectation of good experiences should always be based on expansion. Everything in the Universe moves towards the bigger and moves towards more. Everything in the Universe moves towards greater content.

When you personally don't expand, you slip back into dark energy. What is unique about this is that dark energy is still a usable energy, but not by you and not for your own purposes. When you don't grow, you become fertilizer for somebody else's growth. This is the Law of the Universe, which is the foremost expert on growth and expansion.

A Tenth Part Shared

Therefore, the principle of return is vital. Returning is about substance and is a reciprocal event. It also involves the number 10 or better stated - a tenth part. I don't want to use this space at this time to give you every detail, but I will give you the basics.

Nature is divided up into several biological trophic categories or biological trophic eco systems and is presented in a hierarchal sequence. But this hierarchal sequence does not denote power over the other, but supply to the other. Each level above a previous level comprises only 10% of the previous level in terms of volume, but the previous level is a supply to the next level. This is the basis of energy flow within the Earth.

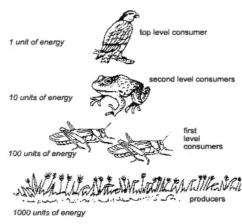

1 unit of energy — top level consumer

10 units of energy — second level consumers

100 units of energy — first level consumers

1000 units of energy — producers

All of this is not a survival system, but a growth system. This serves as a model for what it takes for you to grow to newer levels. What does it take for you to grow to newer, higher, and more expansive levels? Supply. Within this, a tenth part should become a rule of thumb. Not only should you reserve a tenth part of your productivity for the growth of others, but also, you should expect the same of others around you as a return. Life is a continual systemic existence of investments so energy can flow. The people around you should always have a prepared reserve of a tenth part of themselves to push you to the next level. Energy can't be energy without investment and exchange.

If they themselves are not a growing entity, it will be impossible for them to make investments into you. But in the same light, if you make an investment into them with your substantive tenth and they are not growers, their system cannot handle your investment. At this point you cannot expect anything in return.

Expectation must be integral in everything you do. If not, the principle of return becomes impossible to understand. You should always expect results from yourself and the people around you. If you paid $40,000.00 for a car, you would reasonably expect it to run and do its job the first time you drive it. Why when it comes to dealing with people our expectations go out the window?

You should always expect results from yourself and the people around you.

The rule of expectation is also present and not future. That's why evidence is a staple of returning. When you pay $40,000.00 for a car, you are not looking for that car to perform six months from now. You should hold people to the same standards. Development might take time, but performance towards you must be immediate and intimate.

The effects of return are immediate, and you should at least feel them at the level of your inner being. Return leads to awareness of the mechanisms of growth. With this, you are enabled to take advantage of any and all growth opportunities revealed to you. Growth and expansion then become visible to others that might depend on your resulting images to image for themselves and their personal processes. This is why I said that growing is a responsibility. Your success enables the success of others. This is your tenth part and your investment towards life.

Get a clear vision of where you are going. Set yourself up to see what has been provided for your arrangements. Foster the relationships that lead to production. Then enjoy the progression and grow.

Points of Super Significance

I am not a big fan of the word self-esteem, but I do believe that defining ourselves totally happens within us. I also believe that one must believe in himself in order to succeed. But none of this has anything to do with esteem or self-esteem. All of your personal esteem comes from others. Your personal value is not based on how you see yourself, but how others see you and thusly act towards you. Your value is defined by you, but if there are no takers who agree with that definition, then your value is not authenticated.

This is the basis of any economic system. How does a painting gain its value? How is the value of gold assessed? A group or a set of people has to agree that it has value. An artist can say all day long, "my painting is worth a million dollars", but if there is no agreement and action, trade, or return towards that agreement, then the painting is just canvas and ink. The painting thusly carries no significance.

In much the same way, you must value yourself, but if no one around you agrees with that value and then acts accordingly, you will reach a point of insignificance. This is because your value is not authenticated. But here lies the key of responsibility. If the people around you do not pour into you the necessary esteem due to your well-designed self-image and your self-awareness based on good thoughts, then you must change the economy around you. The problem is, is that most people do not account for what's being invested in them by others. You might be a good person that give of yourself to others readily, but if you don't receive a balanced return, it becomes hard to feel significant. There is no balanced system of return in place.

Information, Affirmation, Confirmation

Think of yourself as a coin, of course with two sides. One side is what's in your mind and the other side is what exists outside your mind. Thoughts exist in two dimensions of the same coin. Thoughts in the mind is instant reality and what's outside the mind is also instant reality, but an instant reality designed to be realized through experience. Experience is what determines your value and significance. Experience on the outside only confirms what's in the mind and life is a series of confirmations. Life is about validation.

Life is about validation.

How do you experience your experiences? You experience life primarily through your five senses. But life itself does not start with the five senses. Herein is the issue. A lot of people live life according to their five senses versus using those same senses as a checkpoint to validate their own self-image. This is because there is no light in them. What I mean by that is that there are no ideas, definitions, goals, desires and the like to drive their destiny. Remember, I said to be careful how you start your Day, and that everyday must start with the light of your definitions, which are reminders of who you are and who you are meant to be. Otherwise everything that is done throughout the day will be sensory reactive versus the development of substances that match the good pictures or images within your mind. Anything outside of this will fail.

The five senses are best used as conformation of the proper information from within yourself. The word "attention" here has to be duly noted. What do you pay attention to? Pay attention to what and who pays attention to you. This is vital because you will get a return on what you pay attention to, and this has an impact on your significance in the world.

Pay attention to what and who pays attention to you.

Attention is the beginning of all economics. When the right attention is flowing in two directions, you harness the power of wealth in every area of your life.

Poor

Here's what makes you poor...when it comes to attention from others...

Let me get back to you when I feel like it...
When I get myself together, then I'll see what you need...
I promise you I'll do this for you...
I can't be bothered right now...
I don't get you...
Get back to you later...

Rich

Here's what makes you rich...when it comes to attention towards you...

I know what you are looking for, I'll get right on it...
I see where you are going, what do you need me to do...
Let me take care of that...
I got it done, I knew what you needed...
What can I do to make things better...?

The language and actions that people have towards you should be a confirmation of what you have affirmed within yourself. Confirmations to your affirmations. Your bodies or what I call your existences on earth stem from the thoughts in your mind (two sides of the same coin), but for them to be developed, it has to pass through a system of returning in order to gain value. This is the only way to get a sense of value and significance. We each have our own personal stock exchange that stems immediately outside our thought world. Here are the four attentions that contribute directly to your significance:

The 4 Attentions

The First Attention

The first attention happens in the unseen world of thought. It is "getting" you. It is self-awareness. You must catalog your desires and come up with the clear definitions of who you are. It is also your personal perception. These are your points of affirmation. And you must reaffirm yourself daily! You must have clear affirmations to know what your confirmations towards you have to be. Here, you must give heightened attention to your thought processes by building a portfolio of your mental assets before they hit your personal stock exchange with others.

The Second Attention

The second attention happens in the seen world of existences. It is how you relate to the things and the people around you. It is the awareness of what matches your desires. You must design your physical surroundings to flow with what's in your head and terminate anything that does not correspond, and terminate anyone who doesn't get it. It is accepting your personal provisions. These are also your points of confirmation. And you must have the things and the people in your life to confirm you daily! These confirmations towards you must be clear and accurate and not left in the realm of potential and the hopeful. You must give heightened attention to this initial personal stock exchange so that your personal returns from others have value and significance.

The Third Attention

The third attention happens in the seen world of completions. It is taking stock in your successes and making sure that you are reaching your end goals. It is being aware of the things completed and uncompleted. You must decide by making precise moves towards directions that are set by you and then put in the time to develop what you have decided on without being distracted with things and people who have nothing to do with where you are going. It is your ability to produce. These are the second stages of affirmation. You have to give heightened attention to what's done by you and the people around you. What's done speaks loudly.

The Forth Attention

The forth attention happens in the seen world of growth. Growth is duplicating your efforts effortlessly based on the confirming things and people around you. It is being aware of and taking stock in whether or not you are stuck in one place or stuck on the same level, or whether or not you are constantly and consistently moving forward and gaining new heights. You must be in a state of movement and growth at all times, and then deal with people who are doing the same for themselves and towards you. This is the basis of progression. These are also the second stages of confirmation. Here you have to give heightened attention to your progress.

The 12 Points of Significance

Your personal economy starts with your relationship with others and their relationship towards you. It feels good when people can respond to your needs. Doesn't it? It is even better when people see your needs and respond to those needs without you even having to ask. It is even greater when people can be so tuned into you, that they meet your need before it even becomes a need. This not only gives you significance, but because energy is not spent here, you are immediately enabled to see "the more" in your life and move to your next levels due to people having your back. Every time a need is put to rest, when something is accomplished by partnership, when people agree with you and move in the same direction, and when things are completed, that existence becomes minted or coined into reality.

Your economy starts with your relationship with others.

Whenever you have been rested on one level, the next level is already there waiting for your systemic aggregation of relationships to bring what you're looking for into reality or into the reality of your desired experience – a good experience. True intimacy is not about having to think because your relationship "machine" is so responsive to you, that the difference between thinking and manifesting becomes seamless.

Your five senses should be used as a source of confirmation of these processes and not information for mere survival. When you don't reach for what's inside you to determine your significance, then you reach for things and people outside of yourself to do this job in order to make you feel your significance. Your significance then is at the mercy of other people's behavior verses it being designed by you and then having other people coming into agreement to those designs. You then are not depending on the good information or images from within yourself that will subsequently get confirmation through the five senses, but your senses at this time are used to draw on the experience of things and people in order to fulfill yourself, and this is not a good use of your five senses.

True significance starts on the inside,
then matched on the outside.

Here are the 12 Points of Significance that make up your personal stock exchange that give value to yourself and others:

The 12 Points of Significance

*If You Are Providing These and There are No Returns,
it's not an Investment, Just a Loss!*

1
(To Be Viewed)
The Investment of seeing and knowing a person.

To know a person as in their habits, favorite things, concerns etc.

To be concerned and having a person's back
based on what you see in them.

See, recognize, and care for one's issues.

Everyone needs someone to see and know who they are.

2
(To Be Comprehended)
The Investment of understanding a person.

Understanding of one's issues.

Willing to take in the right information concerning a person.

Agreement and right action towards that understanding of the person.

Everyone has a need to be understood.

3
(To Be Engaged)
The Investment of active commitment.

Physical connection.

Partnership and unification.

Two-way exchange or communication.

Everyone has a need to be touched in some way.

4
(To Be Praised)
The Investment of vocal affirmation of the good.

Recognition and hearing about good attributes.

Complimentary in nature towards a person.

Approvals of ideas, thoughts, visions...etc.

Everyone has a need to hear something good about themselves.

5
(To Be Believed)
The Investment of trust.

Take a position based on concerns verbalized or character exuded.

Action oriented belief qualified by action-oriented support.

Taking responsibility and acting on a person's
behalf based on believing in them.

Everyone has a need to be trusted and believed in.

6
(To Be Prioritized)
The Investment of making one special.

Acute attention in certain situations and areas.

Putting things aside in recognition of the other.

Allowing a person from time to time to be the most important.

Everyone has the need to feel number one sometimes.

7
(To Be Enriched)
The Investment of provision.

Bringing gifts or supplies not associated with earning.

Sharing your personal substance.

Making sure a person's material needs are met.

Everyone has a need to receive.

8
(To Be Advanced)
The Investment of pushing one forward.

Progressing one's effort by means of time and efforts.

Providing leadership in your area of expertise to
advance the cause of another.

To give an effort in setting a situation or circumstance right.

Everyone has a need to be mentored or pushed forward.

9
(To Be Rewarded)
The Investment of recognition.

To provide substance in recognition of what
someone has invested in you.

Physical substance given in appreciation for efforts made
on behalf of the other.

Thank you and appreciation outside of verbal affirmation.

Everyone has a need to be appreciated in a tangible way.

10
(To Be Exalted)
The Investment of one's self into another.

Time spent in all areas of emotional investments.

Giving a sense of place based on your presence.

The gift of yourself that lifts a person to another level,
give status or empowers. Physical praise.

**Everyone has a need to feel another's presence
that builds their own presence.**

11
(To Be Increased)
The Investment of addition.

To empower, enhance, or enable in any way by investing your talent.

To see then add in a positive way time, effort, or substance.

To be an extension for someone where someone comes short.

**Everyone has a need to be completed by the
investment of another's effort and partnership.**

12
(To Be Doubled)

The Investment of multiplication.

The experience of results.

Results that lead to more results.

Results that give a sense of place, home, completeness.

**Everyone has a need to grow by the investment of
another's effort or partnership.**

As you can see; your relationships and how they are set, play a vital role in your ability to see and experience your life in High Definition. This is the true beginning of everything economic. In order to live a fuller and more exciting life, you must prepare yourself to receive your full supply of what's for you by setting your perception in line in order to focus on your own good.

44 Reflection Statements

Perception must start within yourself and there must be a continued awareness of your own personal value. This awareness is maintained by taking your focus off events outside of yourself that might influence your emotion. It is having a "knowing" that extends beyond what you physically see and then building all of your subsequent relationships based on this knowing. By choosing these optimal relationships, you begin to eliminate all the questions that might exist in your life. Your senses are then converted to be used as confirmation instruments to your own good. Remember, the good that you create in your mind is the actual event, and then your experience serves as confirmation to what has been designed by you in your mind. This affords you the opportunity to experience your own existence, which is the essence of a High Definition Life.

Here are 44 reflection statements that are designed specifically to help you to maintain a consciousness of all the processes needed to continue to experience your own well designed and developed existence:

1

"Every-thing" that you need to accomplish "Any-thing",
you already have within you.

2

Take responsibility for your personal development.
The experience of results is the express reason for your existence.

3

There is no financial difference between any human in the world,
only a mind difference.

4

To create, to make something happen, and to produce is spiritual.

5

You must pay attention to the quality of your thoughts.

6

Love is about growing.

7

Things just don't happen to you, they happen from you.
Nothing happens without the mind.

8

Instead of "things" evolving you,
You by design must evolve things.

9

Being able to master your emotions makes you
a master of the Universe.

10

You and your body are designed to produce more of what it is.

11

To determine what something is going to be,
you must set its energy based on who you are.

12

Connection determines energy and energy determines state.

13

Don't become a problem solver, become an idea generator.

14

When you change the energy, you redirect the destiny.

15

It takes relationship to make a true decision.

16

Only the decisions acted on are true decisions.

17

Be a master of what's in your mind and a master of
coming into right agreement with what's outside of your mind.

18

All ends have to match your ends, or you will never reach an end.

19

Without "things" there is no rest.
Wasting your mind is wasting money.

20

Success in life is about creating good memories you can count on.

21

You cannot birth "what's next" without creating "what is" now.

22

To be or not to be is not the question. "You Are" is the answer.

23

Triumph is at the core of all human existence.

24

You must be consistent towards what's on your mind, because you are in a constant state of producing something.

25

People around you should take the energy of who you are and produce more of who you are.

26

People around you must reflect your destination.

27

There is no creation without co-creation.

28

Perception is how you choose to experience the world and the items in it.

29

Perception is our gift to order the very energy of life.

30

Becoming who you are starts with discovering who you are.

31

Clear insight forces foresight.

32

Matching the good in you creates a better world for others.

33

What's outside of you cannot compete with what's inside you.

34

Don't let your dreams die at the next person.

35

Existence must be marked in order for it to be experienced.

36

Your very nature is to expand and grow.
What you produce plays a vital role to all lives
and not just your own.

37

The people you relate to become your story.

38

Choosing relationships should be based on choosing those
who return to you and honor you.

39

Growth is an energy process and anything or
anybody with unlike energy will stunt your own growth.

40

Content has to be the staple of how you value things and people.
Evidence has to play a role in everything you do.

41

You should always expect results from yourself
and the people around you.

42

Life is about validation.
Pay attention to what and who pays attention to you.

43

Your economy starts with your relationship with others.

44

True significance starts on the inside
then matched on the outside through agreement.

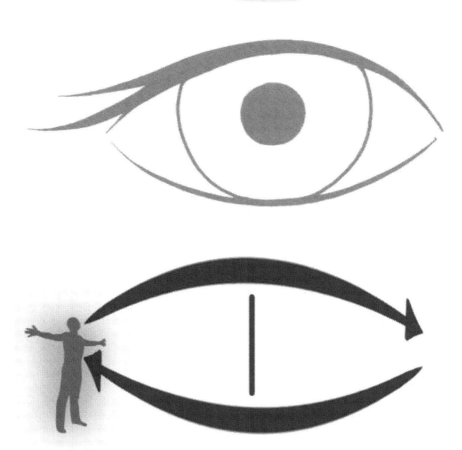

Perception's Eye is a tool that is developed to push you past your current circumstances, issues, and what's not working for you, and then move you rapidly towards your desired goals. But first, the eye has to be developed in stages in order for you to fully comprehend the mechanics of Perception's Eye. Let's start here.

**Current
Issues**

This line represents your current issues or circumstances. Determine what these are and then make specific notes of them. Your current issues can also be noted as your current circumstances, whatever they may be, or your current state - how things are.

The key here is to understand that whatever they are, you are in relationship to those issues. These issues or circumstances can represent the good or the bad, things you like and dislike. Your current issues represent what is present to you in the moment.

It is here that you must determine what your relationships will be, which in turn will subsequently determine your experience. You have full power over this process, but you must be aware of your modes of relationship.

There are two modes of relationship to your current issues or state:

1. CM - Communication Mode

2. EM - Experience Mode

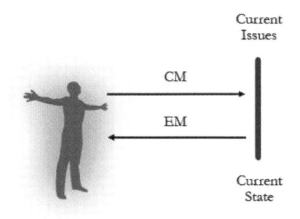

The ***Communication Mode*** consist of four elements of communication that you have with your current state or current issues.

1. Your Thoughts
2. Vocal Communication
3. Action Towards
4. Bodily Energy Directed/Emotional Energy Directed

The ***Experience Mode*** consist of your five senses which determine the rate of your experience. Communication intake.

1. Taste
2. Touch
3. Visual
4. Hearing
5. Smell

Despite your current issue or state, your thoughts, which is a communication mode, precedes all existence. The speed of thought rates faster than the speed of light. There are no issues, circumstances, nor a current state that can interfere with your thought process and your body without you allowing it to do so. The opportunity here is the ability to place within your mind new arrangements of thought. This is:

1. Seeing things differently.
2. Resetting your line of site.
3. Depositing this information in your mind.
4. Reinforcing the information.

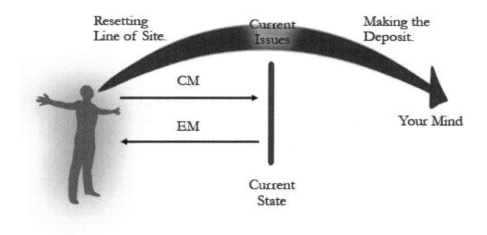

Remember here, that you are thinking beyond your current state, issues, and experience. This information or new arrangements which is what you desire to have or experience, as you are setting these things in your mind, you have to reinforce this information. You have to set up around you reminders of your goals; this can be in the form of writing them down for periodic review, developing story boards, or better yet if available, make a video diary of your goals and watch it daily.

This type of reinforcement is vital because something special is taking place that is paralleling this reinforcement. What is also taking place is the building of parallel structures within your body which becomes your emotional body. What you are building in your mind is also being built in your body simultaneously! This is a biological law and not a philosophical concept.

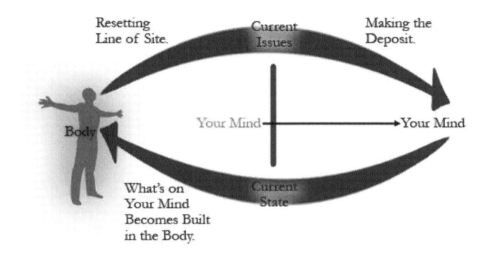

The key here is to consistently move your mind past your current issue or state to a place that only your desire and design can exist. This is a gift and an opportunity. Condition your mind by removing your mind from your condition.

Condition your mind by removing your mind from your condition.

As your new pictures, images, desires, and designs are set into your body, you will be able to tell by your emotions the level in which you are committed to your own ideas. This commitment must now begin to include your other forms of communication modes as you feel the excitement of what you want building up in your body:

1. Vocal Communication
2. Action Towards

This will assist you in solidifying what's on your mind as you set what you say and what you do to follow what is on your mind.

The more powerful this becomes in you, it will begin to set an emotional block to your current issue and state.

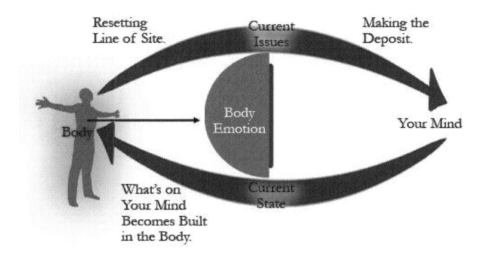

You must realize that the emotional system is the most powerful energy system in the Universe. But it is the system in which we do the least work and arrangements. When your emotional body is this strong, the body will then reflect the supplies for your desires, or better stated - illuminate the supplies for your desire.

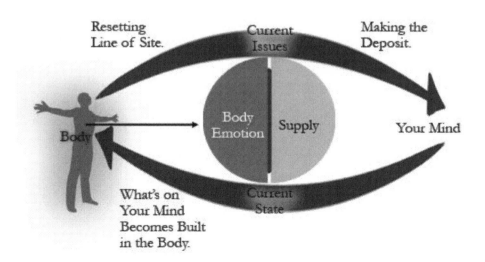

Your emotional system is an antenna and is made to pick up like signals outside of itself for reception. In other words, your emotional system allows you to see the available supplies that are set on your behalf to complete your destiny. Physical supply mirrors your emotions. There are two things that happen to those who build strong emotional content according to their desire:

1. When situations and circumstances shift, the emotions can remain on course. They keep their focus. The house can be on fire, but the emotional resolve is unaffected.

2. They are better enabled to tune into what's for them and they seem to have an endless supply of resources to accomplish their goals.

In actuality, everyone on Earth has an endless supply of resources for any quest or effort to be made. Perception's Eye helps you to bring that supply into your own line of site. Here are some further steps.

1. Develop relationships with people who can fully comprehend what's developed inside you. This becomes easier as your emotional content becomes stronger, because people usually can "feel" you without you having to say much at all.

2. Arrange the supply to build and achieve your desired goals until your outside is in full existence or you reach a stage of completion.

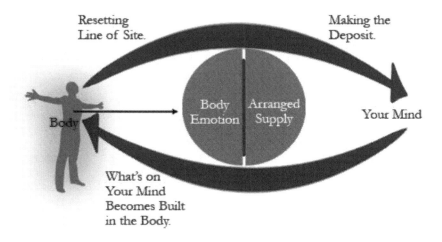

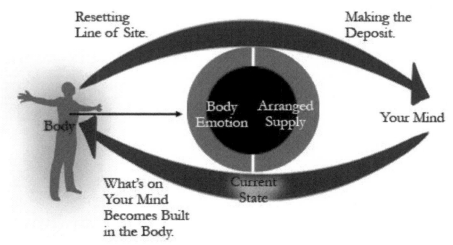

Notice here that the Current State takes on the shape of the combination of what exist inside you and what exist outside of you that is a result of your desire. Here, the Experience Mode is now reflective of who you are, and every part of the Eye becomes single. Your Mind, Your Body, Your Emotions, and Your Experience are all now - One.

After this, new desires are born.

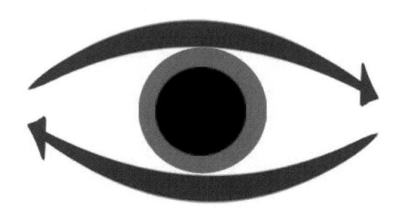

Changing Bad Views

Here's a map of an eye when it is focused on your current issues versus what can be created in the mind that will reflect back to you for your experience. When your issue becomes the focus, the image in your mind is only a mirror of what you see and not something created by you, and the image then contains no substance.

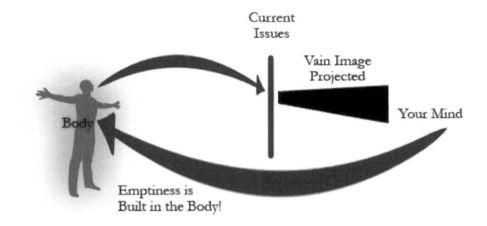

When your issue becomes the focus, this actually blocks your supply.

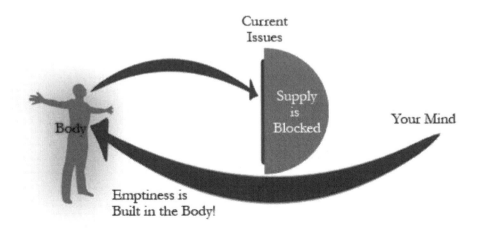

Emptiness is then built into the body. This empty body has no choice but to contain not only the emotions that are reflected from your issues, but the whole process begins to cycle and repeat itself.

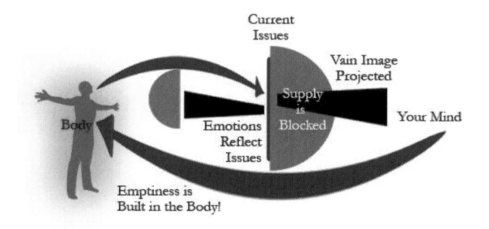

The only solution is to reset your line of site into new creations. These creations are based on your desires and are within your full control.

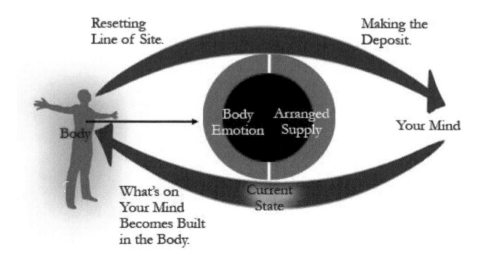

Here are some keys to Perception's Eye for maintaining that control:

Perception's Eye Change Model

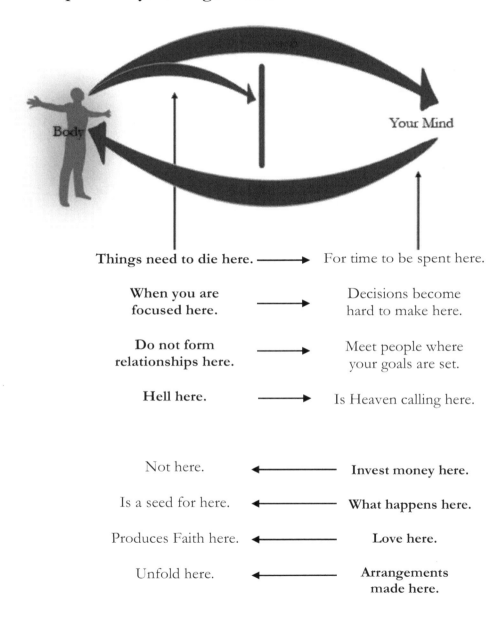

Things need to die here. ———▶ For time to be spent here.

When you are focused here. ———▶ Decisions become hard to make here.

Do not form relationships here. ———▶ Meet people where your goals are set.

Hell here. ———▶ Is Heaven calling here.

Not here. ◀——— **Invest money here.**

Is a seed for here. ◀——— **What happens here.**

Produces Faith here. ◀——— **Love here.**

Unfold here. ◀——— **Arrangements made here.**

Points of Correlation

Principles	Directives	Significance	Attentions
Perception	Desire Design	Viewed Comprehended Engaged	Thought
Provision	Define Determine	Praised Believed Prioritized	Existences
Production	Decide Develop	Enriched Advanced Rewarded	Completions
Progression	Destine Deal	Exalted Increased Doubled	Growth

These are the tools which are set for you to live and experience a High Definition Life. Study them. Use them. Share them. Remember we are gifted with the ability to map out, choose, create, and develop on purpose. With this fact, living a better life becomes a responsibility and a duty.

Triumph is at the core of every human being, but the tools to do so might seem distant to some. If you begin to move towards the life designed for you, the tools will make themselves available to you. This involves sometimes letting some things go, so better things can come. So, see yourself in High Definition so others can witness you in High Definition, which gives them a base to live their life the same - In High Definition.

Made in United States
Orlando, FL
07 February 2024